The Italian-American Child:
His Sociolinguistic Acculturation

Lawrence Biondi, S.J.

Georgetown University Press, Washington, D.C. 20057

Library of Congress Cataloging in Publication Data

Biondi, Lawrence, 1938-
 The Italian-American child: His sociolinguistic acculturation.

 Bibliography: p.
 1. English language in the United States—Dialects—Boston. 2. Italian Americans—Boston. 3. Acculturation. I. Title.
PE3102.I8B5   301.2'1   75-38898
ISBN 0-87840-208-X

Copyright © 1975 by Georgetown University
All rights reserved
Printed in the United States of America

International Standard Book Number: 0-87840-208-X

To my parents
Hugo and Albertina Biondi

Acknowledgments

I am grateful to all of the many people who helped me in so many different ways. A note of thanks is appropriate to the administrators and faculty of the three parochial schools in the North End, and especially to the sixty North End Italian-American children who were my informants and who must remain nameless.

For those who can and should be named, I would like to express my gratitude and appreciation to Professor Roger W. Shuy who represents for me the epitome of the perfect mentor. Dr. Shuy provided needed encouragement and guidance; he gave willingly of his time and generally expedited the progress of the investigation. His patience and availability have been a tremendous help throughout the entire period of research and writing. Very special thanks are due to Professor Ralph W. Fasold for his intellectual honesty and curiosity, especially his willingness to explore, share, and discuss the little achievements and discoveries made at various stages of this study. Dr. Fasold discussed with me often and at great length the problems of variable analysis. His encouragement to tackle head-on the challenges of variable analysis is greatly appreciated. A special debt of gratitude is due to Professor Francis Dinneen, S.J. Father Dinneen's good judgment, instructive editorial comments and suggestions have been a great help.

Among those who assisted in the preparation of this study, credit must also be given to Professor David M. Smith, my former professor of anthropology, who provided initial advice on this topic and wisely guided the preliminary stages of research. I am also grateful to Lucienne Skopek for her very helpful comments and continual support and to Donna Christian for her valuable comments on variable analysis.

I shall always be grateful to my fellow Jesuits at Georgetown University who have helped me in many ways, but especially by their kindness, openness, and generosity. I also deeply appreciate my fellow Jesuits of the Chicago Province of the Society of Jesus who have supported me fraternally and financially during my years of studies in sociolinguistics at Georgetown University.

Contents

1 A Sociolinguistic View of Boston's North End	**1**
General Remarks	1
Research Strategies	3
Theoretical Underpinnings	4
Review of Relevant Research	6
Purpose	9
Procedures: Data Gathering	11
Procedures: Data Extraction	16
Summary	20
2 Boston's North End: A Large 'Little Italy'	**21**
Geography and Population	21
History and Immigration	22
Housing	26
Churches, Schools, and Community Action Programs	28
Market and Restaurants	30
Italian Religious Festivals	31
Crime	33
The Italian-American Community	35
Conclusion	38
3 Variable Analysis of Interdental Fricatives	**39**
General Remarks	39
Word-initial Voiced *th-*	41
Word-medial Voiced *-th-*	44
Word-initial Voiceless *th-*	47
Word-medial Voiceless *-th-*	50
Word-final Voiceless *-th*	52
Correlations with Social Factors	54
Narrative Reading Test	56
Word-pair Reading Test	58
Stylistic Variations	60
Perception-Discrimination Test	63
Summary	66

4 Variable Analysis of Word-Final Consonant Cluster Simplification — 68

General Remarks — 68
Procedures — 69
Constraints on Consonant Cluster Simplification — 71
Correlations with Social Factors — 83
Narrative Reading Test — 84
Stylistic Variations — 85
Summary — 86

5 Variable Analysis of Third Person Singular Present Tense Verb Concord — 88

General Remarks — 88
Irregular Verbs — 89
Regular Verbs — 91
Correlations with Social Factors — 96
Narrative Reading Test — 98
Stylistic Variations — 98
Summary — 99

6 Language Maintenance and Language Shift in the North End — 101

General Remarks — 101
Summary — 111

7 The North End Language Attitudes Study — 112

General Remarks — 112
Purpose and Rationale — 114
Methodology — 115
Results — 120
Summary — 127

8 Summary and Conclusions — 128

The Three Research Questions — 129

Appendix A: Questionnaires — 138

Appendix B: List of Speakers — 148

Notes — 150

References — 151

1
A Sociolinguistic View of Boston's North End

General Remarks

Language is one of the primary tools for discovering the processes involved in socialization not only because language is a central feature of the process itself, but also because language is a singularly accessible form of human communication. One of the most important and recent developments in the field of linguistics has been the development and refinement of descriptive methodologies for dealing with language variability.

This sociolinguistic study of the Italian-American community in the North End of Boston is compatible with the present state of linguistic concerns for a number of reasons. First, there is a current interest among many psycholinguists and sociolinguists in language acquisition and language development with the concomitant recognition that all languages change in response to the demands placed upon them. Secondly, there is an increasing recognition by many anthropologists and linguists that language development involves the interplay between universal, natural linguistic forces and culture specific social pressures. Third, sociolinguistic efforts and resulting variation theory provide preliminary models and paradigms for explaining these processes. Finally, pidgin-creole studies have provided insights into processes of language development and the universal cognitive processes underlying them.

In the broadest sense, problems of education, urbanization, and ethnic relationships can be viewed as communication problems. It is in acquiring communication skills that we develop our perceptual strategies and the abilities to share information with others as we construct and modify our various social institutions. Mastering communication skills involves not only the acquisition of a language but also learning a set of rules governing social interaction including acts of speaking. Inevitably, therefore, their concern for understanding communication must lead investigators to a deeper understanding and greater appreciation of language variability and ethnographies of communication.

An understanding of the sociolinguistic and sociocultural aspects of inter- and intrapersonal forms of communication among North End children is my central research focus. Although no epistemological nor pedagogical salvific formulas result from such a study, since my findings are tentative and exploratory, there are data that point to some interesting implications relating to the processes of acquiring and developing language, bilingualism, and biculturalism, and possibly to language universals and a theory of language. The social factors of age, sex, education, and ethnicity were found to have sociolinguistic relevance when compared to the linguistic variables discussed in Chapter 3, 4, and 5.

Despite the prodigious amount of literature on language acquisition, the process of acquiring communicative competence is still little understood. The notion of competence has been extended from that of the mastery of a set of grammatical rules to that of the mastery of a set of cultural rules (communicative competence) which include the appropriate ways to apply grammatical rules in all speech situations possible for that society (see Hymes 1972). Given the realities of our ethnically heterogeneous, urbanized world, it is insufficient to know, for example, how a child in the North End learns to speak American English. It is just as important to know how he learns the rules of communicative, social interaction including when to say something in English, when not to say it, how to say it, and the various ways of saying the same thing in English.

This study examines the process of language development in monolingual and bilingual Italian-American children in Boston's North End. In this study several terms are consistently used to distinguish between various processes. The term *language acquisition* refers to the process of language development in children. The term *language socialization* refers to the process of learning rules for the linguistic codes of the community (acquisition of communicative competence). Finally, the term *language development* within a specific speech community refers to language acculturation.

The underlying thesis of this work is that language socialization and acculturation are parallel processes subject to normal linguistic constraints. Furthermore, each process profoundly affects the other. This mutual effect is particularly significant and apparent in multi-ethnic urban communities. Therefore, neither language change through time nor language use in a speech community can be understood without an understanding of both of these processes and their interrelationships.

The Italian-American community in Boston's North End provides an excellent opportunity for investigating in a naturally controlled setting the processes of urbanization and inter-ethnic contact as factors in the development of linguistic skills. In addition, the Italian-American setting has offered another important advantage to this type of research. Most of the past studies concerned with language development have dealt with either normal middle class white children or with members of an oppressed minority. As a result it has been tempting to attribute differences in behavior patterns to social stigmatization or oppression. It is my hope that this research has contributed somewhat in clarifying how the ongoing, dynamic processes involved in language acculturation and socialization become interrelated in the linguistic and social development of white, Italian-American bilingual and monolingual children of working-class parents in Boston's North End. This goal is principally carried out by relating the linguistic variables discussed in detail in Chapter 3, 4, and 5 with the sociological variables of age, sex, education level, and ethnicity of the Italian-American children in the North End.

The Italian-Americans in the North End, while numerically a minority, are more powerful and less stigmatized than, for example, Blacks, Puerto Ricans, or Mexican-Americans in other parts of Boston. The Italian-American community has its own political intrastructures and is an important force economically and politically up to the state level. Language acculturation and socialization in the North End community submit to significantly different pressures and social forces than they do in Black, Puerto Rican, and Mexican-American communities in Boston.

Research Strategies

Linguistic descriptive studies and some basic ethnographic work are both necessary in this type of research. In order to discover how monolingual and bilingual North End children acquire a particular set of communication skills, it is first necessary to specify precisely and explicitly what these target skills are. What are the varieties of language an Italian-American child must master in his enculturation, for example? This, of course, involves an even broader question, namely, what are the language codes of this North End community?

A preliminary investigation of the languages spoken in the North End has determined that there are a number of identifiable speech variations in both English and Italian. There are two identifiable and universally recognized social groups, the immigrants from Italy and the American-born. The immigrant population comes from a wide area of southern Italy where numbers of very different regional dialects are spoken. The Italian spoken in Boston represents a mixing or some kind of leveling of these Italian dialects. However, this mixture and its uses have yet to be adequately described. Furthermore, both the native-born Italian-Americans and the acculturated immigrants speak varieties of English which differ from Standard English. Little descriptive work has been done on this and none of it is based on the recent important advances in linguistic theory which are directly concerned with handling variation in the grammar.

Since this study investigates the development of communicative competence, the analysis must specify the rules of social interaction involving the kinds of language variation available to speakers. Who uses a particular variety and under what conditions? What kinds of social statuses or interpersonal relationships is an individual barred from participating in if he does not have certain varieties in his competence? How does competence in certain varieties correlate with and characterize socioeconomic statuses existing in the community? These questions in turn presuppose some understanding of the social structure and culture of the Italian-American community.

The experimental procedures of such research developed concurrently with the ethnographic analysis. The objectives of these procedures are to determine how children acquire the codes with the rules for using them, and to specify the ways in which monolingual and bilingual Italian-American children's linguistic behaviors differ from one another. Such procedures suggest the collection of sociolinguistic data in both controlled and natural settings.

Theoretical Underpinnings

This sociolinguistic study presents an opportunity to test some promising recent developments in linguistic and sociolinguistic theory. Several interrelated major areas of recent theoretical advances are directly important to this investigation.

First, the expansion of linguistic concerns to include more than the analysis of formal linguistic competence is crucial. Linguists of many persuasions are now convinced that an adequate grammar of language must include the rules for generating well-formed sentences and for the kinds of variation which exist in the linguistic competences of individuals as well as in the competences of the speech community. That is, much of what has been traditionally treated as free variation, i.e. variation occasioned by nonlinguistic factors, has now come under the legitimate purview of linguistics.

The second development, which is directly related to the first, is the demonstration that much of the variation in a speech community and in the speech of an individual at different times, is directly determined by social factors. Such factors as the relative social statuses of addressee and addresser, the topic of the message, and the social context of the interaction all affect the choice of the linguistic code. The goal of a truly adequate analysis of the language behavior of a speech community must include an explanation of the variation that exists.

To pursue this goal new models and methodologies in linguistics have had to be developed. Concern with understanding such variation has occasioned a new theoretical orientation—variation theory—that treats both synchronic and diachronic variation as one process. It thus considers as interrelated the variation that exists in a speech community at a given time or change over time, and the differences exhibited by an individual within the community at different times. This is done by positing a set of implicational rules explaining how a variety of speech which correlates with a social status in a given community will, depending on the relative social ranking of that status, either imply the presence (or absence) of this feature in the speech of individuals occupying other statuses or the future adoption (or rejection) of it. For example, if grammatical feature X is found to be used categorically in the speech of people occupying a socially favored social status and variably in the speech of a more stigmatized social group, it will also be found categorically in other still higher classes. Furthermore, the adoption of the feature, at first variably and finally categorically, by the most stigmatized classes, can be predicted. With this model it is thus possible to formulate linguistic rules which not only generate the well-formed sentences of a language but which explain, as well, the presence of speech varieties in a single community.

This model, and the theory of language it embodies, hold great promise for providing powerful tools for analyzing verbal behavior. Empirical studies such as this one on the Italian-American children's linguistic development have hopefully profited from this approach, since it appears best suited to explain the speech behavior of such a community and could serve to test and refine the theory.

As a corollary, the final theoretical development pertinent to this study is, again, closely related to the others. The development of variation theory has proceeded hand in hand with a new appreciation of the significance of pidgin and creole languages. The current concern about understanding the processes of pidginization and creolization stems, at least in part, from the analytical challenges presented by the nature of pidgin and creole languages.

Since traditional techniques of analysis could never account for the nature and functions of these languages, they were long considered too aberrant and too simple to justify attention by serious linguists. It is now recognized that their insusceptibility to analysis did not stem from aberrancy of the language but from inadequacies in the theories of the linguists. In fact, these languages transparently reflect general, natural processes of language development, elsewhere masked by social contingencies.

This fact is consonant with contemporary understanding that language development, both with respect to individuals and speech communities, proceeds in natural universal sequences. Modification, arrest, and even reversal of these procedures can only result from intervention of social forces and can only be of limited scope.

In light of this, it is not surprising to find pidgin and creole languages exhibiting striking similarities to the codes of children at various stages of development, to the codes of language learners in the process of mastering a second language, and to the dialects of communities in the throes of acculturation. Therefore, analyses of the processes of pidginization, creolization, and decreolization may well provide extremely useful models for the general description of language development.

In fact, direct parallels can be drawn between language ontogeny in children and language phylogeny in a speech community. Both the natural processes of language developing from a prepidgin to a postpidgin stage and a child going from a babbling infant to a fully enculturated adolescent, can be seen as progress along continua. In both cases an acrolect, which 'stands for that end of the continuum nearest to English of a creole continuum' (Bickerton 1971) is simplified in form, restricted in function, and intermixed with nonnative elements. The process of development involves elaboration in form, expansion in function, and sorting out of unacceptable features. (The same can be said mutatis mutandis for the process of second language learning.) To be more explicit, as Smith (1973b) points out, initial language learning is ontogenetically parallel to pidginization; language socialization in a child is parallel to creolization and decreolization. Therefore, the understanding of one process has important implications for understanding the other.

Smith (1972:61-77) maintains that where both of these processes are going on concurrently, opportunity exists to examine simultaneously the development of the processes and the relationships they have to each other. Smith contends that this is a significant part of the social process of urbanization. In fact, he would argue that a model of the intersection of the processes of language development ontogenetically and phylogenetically could well provide a paradigm for explaining such urbanization.

In a community like Boston's North End where there is considerable ongoing immigration, it is possible to analyze both processes at various stages. There are cases of early language contact (prepidginization and pidginization) and examples of code elaboration in response to functional demands (creolization and decreolization) in the language community. Likewise, there are instances of individuals at various stages in the process of acquiring communicative competence. Although the pidginization-creolization model of language development could well be a valuable asset for future research in comparing children and adult dialects within the North End community, I have limited myself and focused my attention on the sociolinguistic development of both monolingual and bilingual Italian-American children.

Review of Relevant Research

This review concentrates on recent research on questions of language socialization, particularly in bilingual communities, since that is the concern of this study, and on the sociological literature on Italian-Americans, especially in Boston.

Recent research on how children learn to use language has received impetus from linguists interested in the processes of language change. It has been assumed by generative linguists that real language change, that is, change in competence or change in the grammars that individuals use in a speech community, is normally introduced as a child acquires his native language. One of the first to present this view was Halle (1962). According to his hypothesis, only children have the freedom to reshape their language; adults can only innovate their language.

Later discussions of the role children play in language change, notably those of King (1969) and Kiparsky (1968) elaborated Halle's position, bringing in, for example, the importance of linguistic universals in the development of a child's language competence. More significantly, it was about this same time that scholars working in the area of language variation began to consider several problems related to language socialization. How do children learn not only the language of their community, but also the rules for using it? How do they learn codes, registers, and stylistic variations, for example? Three recent papers which have dealt with these questions illustrate the direction in which this research is going. Berko-Gleason (1971) investigated code-switching in children under five. She discovered that by the age five, children distinguish four categories of addresses: adult friends, adult strangers, peers, and younger children. DeStephano (1972) has made a preliminary attempt to specify how Black children acquire formal register in their speech. Finally, Traugott (1972) in a series of lectures briefly discussed the development of code-switching abilities in her very young daughter. She suggested that an understanding of the variability observable in the speech of very young children would have significant bearing on an understanding of processes of language change.

In a different vein, theoreticians have been concerned with the question of how variability is learned by children with a focus on the variability of adults who make up a speech community. Their interest is in formulating a dynamic theory of language. Weinrich, Labov, and Herzog (1968) attempted to formulate an explicit theory of language change. Bailey (1972) was concerned with the development of a general model of language which would account for synchronic and diachronic variation in the same framework. Smith (1972a) sketched a functional model of language, which viewed language as developing, expanding, and changing in response to social needs. In all three cases the question of how children acquire the rules for using the various codes of their speech community becomes crucial.

Starting with Labov (1966, 1968), followed by Wolfram (1969) and Fasold (1972), to name just three, it has now become commonplace for linguists to include statistically confirmable variation observed in a speech community in their description of grammars. Therefore, while there is considerable debate among these linguists as to the exact implication of their statistics (for example, whether they are to be considered part of an individual's competence or not), models have been developed that include these kinds of data. There is conceptually no reason why they could not be used in the analysis of children's speech.

Sankoff (1972) and Cedergren and Sankoff (1972) have addressed themselves to the problem of developing a usable framework for examining communicative competence. They have concentrated on the necessity for including statistical variation in their approach. The result is a quantitative paradigm that promises to be useful in analyzing data similar to the type this study was designed to elicit.

It is no accident that virtually all of the research in this area, both that designed to further our understanding of language change and that intended to simply further our knowledge of how we learn to use language, has been associated with new interest in pidgin-creole studies. Bickerton, Labov, and Bailey have all been active in this type of research. Sankoff (Sankoff and Kay 1972) is not only working with creole but has also used as primary sources data on French-English bilinguals in Montreal. In addition, Smith has had extensive experience in working with West African pidgin English (Dwyer and Smith 1967; Smith 1972a, 1973b).

The foregoing is representative of the literature concerning linguistic theory and studies relevant to this study. A review of the literature on Italian-Americans reveals, in general, little concern with language problems. However, a number of social issues of direct concern to this research concerning urbanization and socialization are present in the literature. A brief review is presented here.

Of the vast literature on the Italians in America, the one work that is most directly relevant to this study is that by Herbert Gans, *The Urban Villagers* (1962). In this study, Gans attempted a fairly comprehensive analysis of the social structure of the North End community. He discovered that in Old Italian settlements, like the North End, the social structure is essentially an accommodation of southern Italian peasant patriarchal family orientation to the exigencies of an American urban context. The result is a system based on strong feelings of community and a pervasive ethnic consciousness cutting across traditional village loyalties.

According to Nelli (1970:78), 'this was not an old world transplant but a new development of the new world.' The presence of this type of cultural accommodation or creolization has been dealt with extensively in the literature (Lopreato 1970: De Conde 1971). Very little, however, has been said with respect to language processes and, in turn, the relationship of language acculturation to social mobility. Attention has focused on the family, religion, political, and economic systems.

MacDonald and MacDonald (1962) investigated the operation of the *Padrone* system as a factor in cultural development among Italian-Americans. This system was a significant factor in determining the distribution of immigrants in the United States and in promoting urban settlements (Iorizzo 1970). It was also important in ensuring that most immigration was from the culturally and economically poor heterogeneous part of southern Italy. The MacDonalds indicated that later the *Padrone* system, which often resulted in virtual indenture and inevitably impoverished living conditions, was superseded by a kind of chain migration which saw many immigrants encourage and help relatives or friends, often with the result that families were at least temporarily split up.

The result of these factors was a dramatic change in family importance (Campisi 1948). Campisi looked at first and second generation Italian immigrants, comparing family composition and size, roles and statuses, interpersonal relationships, marriage and birth practices, sexual attitudes, and so on, and discussed the psychological results of family acculturation on individuals. His 1948 results corroborate my observations that first generation families tend to react negatively to perceived permissiveness and withdraw so that peer, friend, and strangers' influence on children is limited. Furthermore, he reported different attitudes for parents and children regarding language shift.

Palisi (1966) also reported that after the first shock of entry, friends replace family in the most important interpersonal behaviors. He also concluded that first an extended family structure replaces the important nuclear family structure of southern Italy, and then this structure is gradually superseded by a network of friends patterned after the American model.

Gambino (1974) wove together the history, sociology, and psychology of first, second, and third generation Italian-Americans. According to Gambino, the twenty million or so Italian-Americans in the United States today have come to be one of the most maligned and misunderstood ethnic groups in America. Gambino also revealed the psychological dilemma of the third and fourth generation Italian-Americans who seem to be undergoing a significant identity crisis. He pointed out that blame is heaped upon their parents who continue to bear their childhood burden of wearing two masks: Italian within the environment of the home and American everywhere else. According to Gambino, this double identity of living on the margins of two cultures has unintentionally confused their children with their seemingly contradictory wishes. On the one hand, second generation parents encourage their children to get an education so that they can be upwardly mobile while, on the other hand, they warn their children not to change their attitudes and life-styles. Gambino is of the opinion that by expecting their children to maintain the precarious balance of conflicts that has become the life-style of their own second generation, they are accentuating the cultural isolation and social loneliness which many third generation Italian-Americans experience when they attempt to enter the mainstream of American life.

In addition to family changes, religious acculturation has been described (Tomasi 1970, Vecoli 1969, Russo 1970, and Banfield 1958). Each study demonstrates that the culture systems of the Italian-Americans, reflected in their living patterns, are both an accommodation to American urbanization and a mixture of diverse elements from the Old World.

Despite the obvious interest this ethnic community should hold for linguists, surprisingly little has been done to describe the linguistic acculturation of the Italians, especially as they relate to these other acculturative developments. This is particularly astonishing for communities with as much promise of fruitful research as the one under consideration here, with its interaction of both acculturation and socialization. The attitudinal and social forces exerted by the ethnicity and urban character of Boston's North End community provide an excellent opportunity to specify how these various influences interact in the development of communicative competence.

Purpose

The purpose of this study, therefore, is to investigate the manner in which monolingual and bilingual children of the North End Italian-American community speak English and the manner in which they learn the rules for social interaction in an acculturating community. An examination of three linguistic variables and of the processes of language socialization and acculturation are made to understand the linguistic development and socialization of these children. In order to determine the underlying linguistic and socialization processes of these children, three research questions are dealt with in this study.

   1. How are Italian and/or English used by monolingual and bilingual children in the North End community?

The population selected to investigate this question consists of sixty monolingual and bilingual children drawn from the same socioeconomic level of working-class parents. The majority of the children's mothers are either housewives or textile factory workers and the fathers are well-paid construction workers or are workers in comparable positions. Data were elicited from the sixty informants during the tape recording sessions concerning the language they use, when, where, and with whom. In addition, questionnaires were used to assess the children's attitudes toward language shift and maintenance and the use of English and/or Italian. These data were supplemented and checked by participant observation in the life of the community. The participant observation method produced additional data on language use. It permitted a check on the accuracy of the informant's impressions as to when he uses one language as opposed to the other and it also permitted the observation of stylistic or other socially determined code changes of which the speaker is unaware. Furthermore, this part of the data gathering procedure permitted an accurate description of the social structure of the community. The samples of speech were analyzed with two goals in mind: (1) to analyze the differences in the speech of new immigrant children born in the North End of immigrating parents as compared to those children who have been born in the North End of American-born parents; and (2) to compare the variations associated with social factors, for example, context of the utterance, age and sex of the speaker, and the topic of the speech act. Variable rules were formulated to account for the variations observed.

   2. What are the linguistic differences between American English speech of monolingual children and bilingual children with respect to various social factors such as grade-age, sex, and ethnicity?

Analyses were done on the English language samples of both monolingual and bilingual Italian-American children and comparisons were made on specific linguistic variables, and specific linguistic and social settings. Furthermore, comparisons were made between the language descriptions of both monolingual and bilingual children of various ages. The significant questions which were answered are: (1) To what degree does the English of monolingual children differ from that of bilingual children? (2) Are there linguistic features which are categorically or variably absent in one but present in the other? (3) Does the English of assimilated children have fewer categorical Italian features than that of nonassimilated children? (4) Does the English of the most assimilated speakers in both categories contain more marked features both categorically and variably than that of less assimilated speakers? Such comparisons show whether the changes children introduce in the language, in multi-ethnic situations, are in the direction of more markedness rather than less markedness, which is presumed to be the case in homogeneous speech communities.

    3. What is the influence of language attitudes and language usage on the Italian-American children's acculturation and socialization processes?

Comparisons were made between the amount of use of English and attitudes toward English, and the amount of contact with non-Italians. The significant questions which were answered are: (1) To what extent are monolingual and bilingual children being socialized into the North End community? (2) What influence does the constant in-migration of southern Italian families with minimal competence in English have on both monolingual and bilingual children? (3) Do newly arrived families find themselves split attitudinally? (4) Do immigrant parents view the democratic family structures of the United States as permissive and a threat to their own way of life? (5) Do immigrant parents consequently become more conservative and withdrawn from social contact than in Italy? (6) Do these parents view learning English as a threat and so have strong attitudes toward maintaining Italian for themselves and their children? (7) Do bilingual children view learning English as a means to escape the oppressive paternalism within the home environment? (8) Do bilingual children use English as much as possible in order to enter into and become accepted by the monolingual youth culture of the North End?

Procedures: Data Gathering

There are four elementary schools in the North End; three are Roman Catholic and one is public. The three Catholic schools, St. Mary, St. Anthony, and St. John, all have grades one through eight. The only public school in this area, Eliot, has grades one through six only. It was necessary to exclude the Eliot elementary school as a potential source for informants because the research design, being developmental in scope, was bent on discovering potential sociolinguistic factors of the grade school children as they begin their elementary educational years as well as those who are about to end it. In addition to these students in either the first or eighth grades, the fourth grade was chosen as the midpoint or median grade level of the elementary school years, again to have a fixed point in comparing the beginning, middle, and end periods of development along the linguistic and socialization continua. Thus the parochial schools were the only possible schools in the North End area for such a study.

The principals of the three schools were originally contacted by telephone; appointments were made with each principal to explain in greater detail the scope of the sociolinguistic research project, to clarify the method of interviewing the grade school children, and to offer any possible services on my part for the benefit of the school administrators, faculty, or students. Each principal was told the purpose and scope of the research project, namely, the investigation of the sociolinguistic principles at work in (1) Italian-born or Italian-speaking children living in the North End whose parents were born in Italy but immigrated to the North End, and (2) American-born and therefore American English-speaking monolingual children living in the North End whose parents were also born in the North End. These, then, were the two large categories of all of the sixty informants. The *first* category of informants were children who were either born in Italy, and perhaps may have spent some of their early childhood years in Italy, and then immigrated with their parents to the North End, or children who were born in the North End of recent immigrating parents. The children in category one spoke both Italian and English. The *second* category of informants were children who were born in the North End and whose parents were born in the North End. Although children in category two spoke only English, the majority of their parents can speak both English and Italian. However, when communicating with their children, only English was used by bilingual parents. Predictably, all children in category one are bilingual speakers of both Italian and English whereas all children in category two are monolingual speakers of English. Henceforth, children in category one will be referred to as *bilingual* Italian-Americans and children in category two as *monolingual* Italian-Americans.

All three principals permitted examination of the school records in order to establish which students could be potential informants for either of the two categories. The elementary school records for the Archdiocese of Boston provide information regarding: (1) the student's name, address, telephone number, date and place of birth; (2) the student's mother's maiden name, place of birth, and occupation; and (3) the student's father's name, place of birth, and occupation. These school records greatly facilitated the process of differentiating potential informants into either category one or category two.

Twenty students from each of the three grades were considered an adequate representative number. Ten of the twenty informants in each of the three grades were from category one and the remaining ten were from category two. Furthermore, five of the ten students in each of the two categories were boys and the other five were girls. The schema of all sixty informants is shown in Table 1.1.

Table 1.1. Comparison of sixty North End informants according to grade, sex, and ethnicity

	I Bilinguals		II Monolinguals	
	Males	Females	Males	Females
First	5	5	5	5
Fourth	5	5	5	5
Eighth	5	5	5	5

1 A sociolinguistic view of Boston's North End / 13

All potential monolingual and bilingual Italian-American children in the first, fourth, and eighth grades from all three parochial schools were selected by random sampling. When the class lists for all students in each of the three grades were studied in relationship to their sexual identity, ethnicity, and place of birth, and the place of birth of their parents, random sampling was then used to determine the five potential informants required to complete each cell shown in Table 1.1. St. Anthony's school tended to have a larger representative sampling of informants. This was due to St. Anthony's relatively larger student enrollment compared to either St. Mary's or St. John's.

The pilot study of the research design was tested for a period of two weeks. The results of the pilot study were then analyzed and corrections were made to improve both the method and chronological sequencing of various administered sociolinguistic tests as well as the general methodological procedures of using various interviewing techniques in order to elicit casual, narrative, or free-style speech samples. The eight-part interview for each of the sixty informants lasted an average of fifty minutes. The period of time needed to complete the entire research project in which all the data were collected was approximately ten weeks.

The first part of the interview consisted in putting the informant at ease emotionally. When each child came to the conference room, I introduced myself and explained how I came to choose him or her. I further explained that, not being from the North End, I was interested in knowing what North End kids like to do in the neighborhood; what they thought of the summer religious festivals; how they felt about the Italian and English languages spoken in the North End. I asked each informant if he or she did not mind telling me about these and similar things, and if I could tape record his or her answers. I tried to appear as non-threatening as possible. No child responded negatively to my request to tape record his or her answers. Two children, however, one girl in the first grade and one girl in the fourth grade, seemed so nervous and so reluctant to speak freely during the first ten minutes of the tape recording session that I decided to conclude the interview for their benefit. I then had to select two other potential informants by random sampling in order to replace the two nervous children.

The second part of the interview consisted of the actual conversation-type interview. The questions used in this part of the interview to elicit casual speech were adopted from Fasold's study (1972:239-240) with specific modifications for the North End children (see appendix A). The various topics for discussion were not always adhered to faithfully for not every informant was asked the same question. Rather a typical conversation-type interview consisted of digressions, questions asking for more details on a given topic, clarifications, or follow-up questions on some obvious hobby or interest indicated by the informant during the course of the conversation. For example, the pilot study suggested the strong interests of all three grade levels. When first graders were asked what their favorite television programs were, many of these children answered: 'The Three Stooges,' 'The Brady Bunch,' 'The Partridge Family,' and 'The General Electric Show.' Fourth graders, on the other hand, when asked, What movie have you seen recently that you liked? would respond, 'The Sound of Music.' Fortunately, all the fourth grade children of all three schools had recently participated in a field day to view this film. Consequently, the fourth graders were able to remember the film's story and so narrate the events in great detail. Eighth graders indicated a wider range of likely conversational topics: boy-girl relationships, high school aspirations, parental authority problems, and suspense-thriller type of films. All the eighth grade boys talked enthusiastically about the Boston Bruins hockey team while the girls talked about the latest fashions and designs in women's clothing.

After fifteen to twenty minutes of eliciting casual speech during the recording part of the interview, I deliberately interrupted the question-and-answer, spontaneous type of conversation. I then asked each informant to listen to a cassette tape. The prepared tape for this third part of the interview consisted of forty randomly selected assorted pairs of words exemplifying both voiced and voiceless interdental fricatives in initial, medial, and final positions (see appendix A). The task for each informant was to discriminate pairs of words as sounding the same or as sounding different. The motivation for interrupting the flow of casual, or spontaneous speech was to prevent the informant from becoming too tired or bored with any one task. The need to switch to some task became a rather obvious conclusion from the pilot study, especially with the first and fourth grade children. A brief explanation of this task of discriminating pairs of words was given to each informant. I then played the tape on which another Standard English speaker from Chicago, Illinois, gave similar instructions (see appendix A). I then stopped the tape and answered any questions, often times explaining and distinguishing the differences between the rhyming of two words and the similarity of sounds of two words. The informant then listened to each pair of words and had to decide if a given pair of words sounded the same or sounded different. The informant was told to listen to any significant difference between two words. The informant was then to circle the letter, S, if the pair of words sounded the *same*, or D, if the pair of words sounded *different.*

After this perception/discrimination test of interdental fricatives, I asked each informant to read a short selection. I taped the informant's reading selection which was chosen for his or her appropriate grade level (see appendix A). This fourth part of the interview usually lasted two to three minutes, depending on the length of the reading passage and the speed of reading the passage.

The fifth part of the interview consisted in the continuation of the elicited casual type of speech. The variety of tasks in parts three and four facilitated the easy entry into the casual, or narrative, speech sampling. This fifth part usually took about ten minutes.

In the sixth part, I asked the informant to read the same list of forty pairs of words as in part three. It was hoped that the intervening parts of the interview were sufficiently varied to distract the informant from remembering what he or she had heard in the perception-recognition test of the interdental fricatives in part three. When asked if the list of words which the informant had just read was similar to the one he or she had to discriminate as same or different, the majority of the students answered that the two lists seemed quite different. Only one informant, an eighth grade monolingual male, said the list seemed almost identical except for a few pairs of words. The same list of words for both tasks of comprehension-discrimination and production was kept for comparative measurement purposes. It should be noted here that only the fourth and eighth grade children read the list of interdental fricative pairs of words. The first grade children had confirmed in the pilot study the expectation that they would find reading this list a tedious task, if not an outright impossibility. Therefore, this selection alone was the only part of the entire data gathering interview session which was omitted by the first graders. All other tasks were commonly shared by all first, fourth, and eighth grade children.

Once the thirty minute recording session was concluded, I asked each informant in the seventh and final part of the interview for information on the Personal Data Information questionnaire (see appendix A) both to confirm the already received information from the school's records and to receive supplementary information such as the number of siblings and so on. I then administered two other questionnaires: one to discover the degree of usage of Italian inside and outside the home; and the other to establish the facts concerning the maintenance of Italian or shift to English (see appendix A). If any question in the questionnaires was unclear, I paraphrased the question until it was understood by the informant. All three questionnaires in this seventh part usually took ten minutes to complete. The entire seven-part interview for each informant generally lasted fifty to sixty minutes.

During the final week of gathering sociolinguistic data in the North End, the Language Attitudes Study test (see appendix A) was administered to all fourth and eighth grade children in each of the three parochial schools. The number of students taking this language attitudes test totalled 148. The twenty informants representing the fourth grade and the twenty informants representing the eighth grade were also part of this total 148. However, the first grade children from all three schools had to be excluded from this test because of the test's relative complexity as well as its form. The pilot testing of this language attitudes test confirmed the suspicion that it would be too difficult for the majority of the first graders.

The language attitudes test consisted in listening to a cassette tape recording of twelve different speakers. The fourth and eighth grade North End Italian-American children were asked to listen carefully to each of the twelve speakers and then to answer a set of identical questions for each of the twelve speakers. These twelve speakers were white and black boys and girls from either Boston's North End, Detroit, or Washington, D.C. The twelve speakers on the tape were randomly chosen and ordered from previously recorded North End children, from Shuy's Detroit Dialect Study tapes, and from spontaneous speech samples of Washington, D.C. grade school children.

Procedures: Data Extraction

After examining the variety of data culled from the pilot study, it was apparent that the data yielded a number of potential linguistic variables. However, keeping in mind the realistic and feasible scope of the sociolinguistic research for a doctoral dissertation, the author decided to delimit an in-depth investigation to three linguistic variables: (1) the voiced and voiceless interdental fricatives; (2) word-final consonant cluster simplification; and (3) concord of a third person noun or pronoun with the third person singular present tense verb. The decision to analyze these three variables was based principally on the sociolinguistic fact that judgments which are made about a person's social status on the basis of his speech typically depend on the frequency of occurrence of certain linguistic features and also the combinations of features which occur in his speech. Therefore, the author decided to analyze these three linguistic variables on the basis that they are indeed socially significant and that they had high frequencies of occurrence in the speech of the North End children. If a thorough contrastive analysis of English and Italian were the author's goal, then he would have had to present an all-inclusive study of the phonological, morphological, and syntactic similarities and dissimilarities of these languages. However, the author judged that for the sociolinguistic goals of his investigation, which were to determine the linguistic development and socialization of the North End children, it became necessary that only those linguistic variables having a strong social significance would be investigated.

In analyzing each of the three linguistic variables, if there happened to be more than one example of the kind of form being extracted, the sentence would be written as many times as there were forms, following Fasold's clear and precise methodology of extracting data (1972:29-32). For example, if an Italian-American child were to say: *So they said everyone could climb up there so they could get to the engine room*, with four examples of voiced interdental fricatives, the sentence would be written on four separate cards—two for *they*, one for *there*, and the final one for *the*. Each card was then coded along the upper left or right hand sides and top edge of the four by six card representing various categories which were considered to be of interest and importance with regard to the particular feature under question. For example, the first inch on the upper left-hand side of the card, that is, on the left side edge of the card, was designated as the field for the presence or absence of voiced interdental fricative //d//. If the sentence on the card contained an example of the voiced interdental fricative, this field was then marked by coloring it with a red felt-tip marker indicating the expected, intact feature. However, if the variable feature of the voiced apico-alveolar stop //d// was present, this field would then be colored with a black felt-tip marker indicating despirantized //d//. In addition, the six fields along the top edge of the card designated both preceding and following environments such as vowels, consonants, and sentence boundary as well as specific kinds of consonants such as sonorants, spirants, and stops, and so on. With such a method developed and perfected by Fasold, it was rather easy to extract the data from the cards as well as to check out various possible linguistic constraints. Commenting on this method, Fasold says:

> This system had the effect of encouraging the investigation of a number of hypotheses, since checking a new hypothesis did not require a time-consuming and mind-numbing eyeball search of hundreds of cards. Even if the cards had not been coded for precisely the kind of information required by a hypothesis which was thought of after the data had been extracted, it was usually the case that they were coded for something which would cut down the number of cards which would have to be actually read... The fact that hypotheses come to mind after the data are extracted shows why it is very desirable to extract data by a method which makes all relevant information recoverable. (Fasold 1972:30)

Figure 1 schematically illustrates a sample card for the voiced interdental fricative.

Figure 1. Sample data extraction card

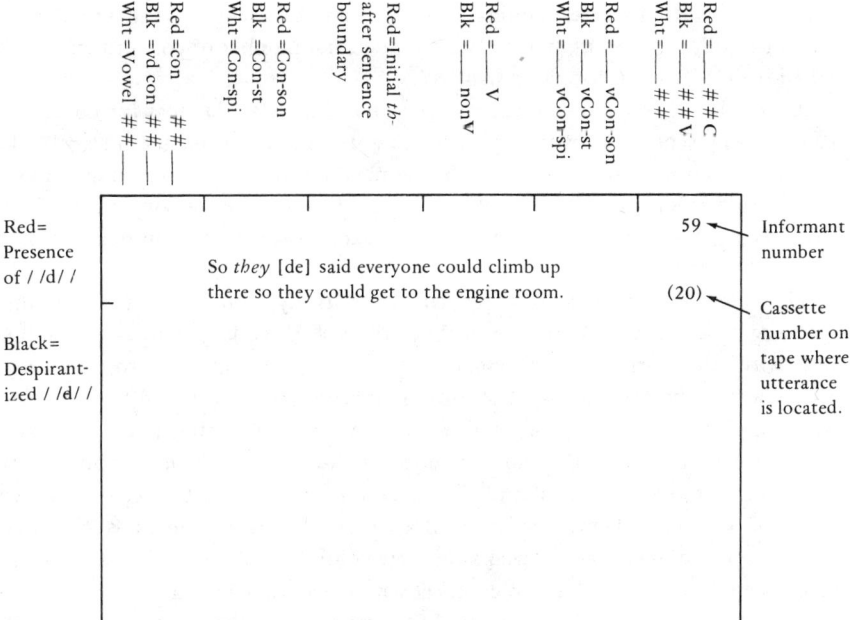

The actual work of extraction was done by me. I decided to extract from each informant a certain number of examples according to the linguistic variable under investigation. For the voiced interdental fricative feature appearing in initial position, I decided to extract ten examples but no same word with initial voiced *th-* would be collected more than two times. For voiceless interdental fricative in word initial position, again ten examples were collected with a maximum number of three examples for any one word. For medial position *-th-* exemplifying both voiced and voiceless interdental fricatives, a limited number of ten examples were gathered of which any given word with medial $//ð//$ or $//θ//$ would be collected not more than three times. For final *-th*, once again ten examples were the maximum number collected with any one word not counted more than three times. Therefore, the outside possible number of examples that any one informant could give for both voiced and voiceless interdental fricatives appearing in initial, medial, and final positions would be sixty examples. However, the total number of examples for all sixty informants for all the above possible positions was 2,066. In analyzing the spontaneous speech of all sixty informants' recorded speech, only two examples of the voiced interdental fricative in final position were found.

The second linguistic variable under investigation was word-final consonant cluster simplification. Twenty examples of this variable were collected from each informant. Any one word illustrating the presence or absence of this variable was not used more than two times. The total number of examples for word-final consonant cluster simplification was 822.

The third linguistic variable was concord of third person singular present tense verb with a corresponding noun or pronoun. Again, the number of examples collected was limited to twenty; the total number of concord examples culled from all sixty informants was 287.

Although a given number such as ten or twenty was the goal for collecting samples representing a given linguistic variable, some informants did not yield the desired number of examples. The number ten or twenty served as a loose control, following Fasold's suggestion (1972:32), to make the longer interviews more manageable and to keep the more loquacious speakers from being grossly overrepresented.

The use of statistics has played a relatively important role in this sociolinguistic study, not only in dealing with the three linguistic variables, but also with the various questionnaries and tests administered to the sixty informants. The chi-square test for independence of variables was used frequently in Chapters 3, 4, and 5. The X^2 test is a statistical procedure frequently used to test the independence of two characteristics. Suppose, for example, that one wishes to study the relationship between hair color and eye color of women. From a suitably drawn sample each woman is classified according to her hair color as well as her eye color. The observed frequencies can be presented as in Table 1.2, which is known as a contingency table.

Table 1.2 indicates that there were 32 women in the sample who were both blue-eyed and light-haired; 22 women who were both brown-eyed and dark-haired, and so on. The table also shows that there were 52 light-haired women in all, 44 blue-eyed women, and 95 women in the entire sample. The

Table 1.2. Correlation of light- or dark-haired women having blue, brown, or other colored eyes

Hair color		Eye color	Blue	Brown	Other	Total
	Light		32	14	6	52
	Dark		12	22	9	43
	Total		44	36	15	95

above table is called a 2 x 3 table since it has two rows and three columns of entries. In this setting the term 'independence' means that the distribution of one characteristic should be the same regardless of the other characteristic. For example, if eye color and hair color are independent, then the proportion of blue-eyed women having light-colored hair should be the same as the proportion of brown-eyed women having light-colored hair. The X^2 statistical test examines the proportions in the same way and determines whether they are significantly different. If they are significantly different, then one can reject the assumption that the two characteristics are independent.

The X^2 statistic for any general r(ow) by c(olumn) contingency table can be calculated. This number is compared against a critical number, the values of the X^2 statistic with $(r-1) \times (c-1)$ degrees of freedom. In testing hypotheses it is customary to choose p to be 0.05 or 0.01 when finding the critical value. As used in this study, with each statistic calculated from a contingency table there is associated a probability or level of significance. If for a given table we calculate that $p < .05$, this means that we have at least a 5 percent level of significance. The exact interpretation of this level is: if we conclude that the characteristics in question are *not* independent, then the probability that we are in error in making such a judgment is less than 5 percent. Thus, the smaller the value of p, the more confidence we can have in rejecting the idea that the characteristics are independent. The results of a test are said to be *significant* if we can reject the idea of independence with a level or value of $p < .05$. It is considered *highly significant* if it is rejected with the value of $p < 0.01$.

It should be noted that rejecting the fact of independence does not automatically give one the direction of the dependence, nor does it really tell us the degree of dependency. It is sometimes stated that the X^2 test can be applied to determine whether there is any association between variables. Association is a more general term than correlation in that it applies to nominal as well as numerical data.

The statistical results from computerized tabulated questionnaires such as the language maintenance and language shift, language usage questionnaires (Chapter 6), and the language attitudes test (Chapter 7) greatly facilitated in objectifying in greater detail the relevant implications of correlated linguistic and social factors. Statistical applications have helped to indicate and discriminate those sociolinguistic areas of high significance.

Finally, it is assumed that the reader is familiar with the type of variable analysis typified in Labov (1966) or Wolfram (1969), and particularly, the formal representation of variable constraints suggested by Labov et al. (1968), Labov (1969), Wolfram (1974), and Fasold (1970, 1972). It is also assumed that the reader is familiar with generative-transformational grammar (particularly, the phonology of Chomsky and Halle's *The Sound Pattern of English* (1968), whose phonological system is used in this volume, and the grammar of Chomsky's *Aspects of the Theory of Syntax*), the theoretical model which serves as a basis for rule formalization.

Summary

The character of the North End has made it an interesting, natural laboratory for the kind of sociolinguistic research undertaken in this study. The North End is typical of many ethnic enclaves in its makeup and yet it is limited enough to have made practical research possible. Its long history of Italian settlement with its present influx of immigrants has enabled linguistic variables to be examined and correlated with social factors such as grade-age, sex, and ethnicity. Italian-Americans are an important group to study in terms of general principles of socialization and acculturation. They are also a significant minority in their own right, and as such, the results of this study will hopefully be somewhat useful for educators of North End children who might need to understand and appreciate the ongoing dynamics at work with language variability in the linguistic development and socialization of the monolingual and bilingual Italian-American children living in the North End of Boston.

2
Boston's North End: A Large 'Little Italy'

I like the North End because everybody helps one another. Everybody knows each other. It's like a big family around here. There's a lot of Italians around here too. And all the kids in the North End all help each other; if you're in a fight, your friend will help you out. It's safe here in the North End; you can walk down any street at two o'clock in the morning and no one will bother you, if you're from the North End. If someone isn't from the North End and he's making trouble, he'd better watch out 'cause we'll take care of him. That's one thing we don't need—no police. We take care of our own situations; like there's not really any riots; you don't hear of no one snatching people's purses or really nothing like that.

The speaker is a fourteen-year-old boy attending the eighth grade at St. Anthony's Grammar School. His views come close to representing the consensus of 12,000 residents of this tight little cultural island of Italians. The North End is Boston's Italian quarter, a closed city within a city. The North End is a well-defined area; it is only three-quarters of a square mile, approximately twenty-five acres, and it is tucked away in the farthermost corner of Boston. Surrounding the North End, similar to the famous walled, island-like Italian city of Lucca in Tuscany, are the waterfront of Boston's harbor and the Central Expressway. In order to understand better this Italian-American community, let us first examine its ethnic composition. The present ethnography of the North End in Boston is the synthesis of the data found in a five-month long ethnographic field work investigation of this densely populated quarter dubbed by Bostonians 'Little Italy.'

Geography and Population

North Enders enjoy and take pride in their geographic insular location. Bordered on three sides by the Charles River and on the fourth by the elevated, aerial ribbon of steel, concrete, and asphalt of the Central Expressway, the North End residents think and feel protected from what lies beyond these enclosing barriers: the impersonal modernization of the downtown area; crowded high-rise commercial buildings; congested wholesale meat and produce markets; old, dilapidated factories, warehouses, and wharves which line the harbor section of the North End; and Boston's massive Government Center complex. Government Center was once the West End where many Italian-Americans lived in tenement houses similar to the tenements in the North End. The West End was declared a slum in 1953. It was torn down under the federal renewal program between 1958 and 1960, and its Italian-American residents dispersed all over the Boston Metropolitan area. During the early and mid-1960s, government buildings were erected in this area once known as the West End. Herbert J. Gans wrote *The Urban Villagers* (1962) in which he describes the ethnic makeup of the West End and its low-income population.

Within the North End's geographical boundaries (roughly similar in size to the area of the Boston Common plus the Public Garden) live approximately 12,000 permanent residents; 89.0 percent of these residents are Italian-Americans either by Italian birth or extraction (Dunn 1973:20). This characteristic gives the North End its special quality, for nearly all North Enders are related to one another by blood, marriage, or most commonly, by ancestral roots in particular districts of Italy's southern provinces. North Enders are Boston's most homogeneous ethnic group. This area has become home away from home for thousands of Italian-Americans who live in suburbia or in other parts of Massachusetts and New England. Many Italian-American families return faithfully each year to the colorful and crowded summer festivals. The large number of permanent residents make the North End one of the largest urban areas, second only to Calcutta, India in population density (Tramontozzi 1972:56). Even though the narrow twisting streets contribute to the noisy traffic congestion, visitors and tourists are amazed to see drivers double park their cars or trucks and then simply walk away indifferently. A true picture of the prevailing congestion cannot be sketched without noting the dozens upon dozens of buildings and areas used for purposes other than residential: innumerable delicatessens, butchers shops, seafood stores, pastry shops, and restaurants. In addition, there are three high schools, a vocational training school, four grade schools, six churches, and a handful of single-lot playgrounds along with the well-known historical sites—all located within an area three-quarters of a mile square.

History and Immigration

Sooner or later everyone living in or visiting Boston hears of the famed Freedom Trail walk. Sidewalks with red painted footprints or single red bricks down the center of the sidewalk guide the curious pilgrim of pre-Revolutionary history to Boston's many historical sites. According to the Massachusetts State House statistics, 450,000 tourists from all parts of the United States and abroad follow the Freedom Trail of historical landmarks which begins at the State Capitol Building and ends at the Old North Church in the North End (Tramontozzi 1972:56). The North End is one of the oldest and most famous historic areas in the United States; it rests on a large portion of the heart and soul of colonial-Revolutionary old Boston. Every American school boy or girl

2 Boston's North End: A large 'Little Italy' / 23

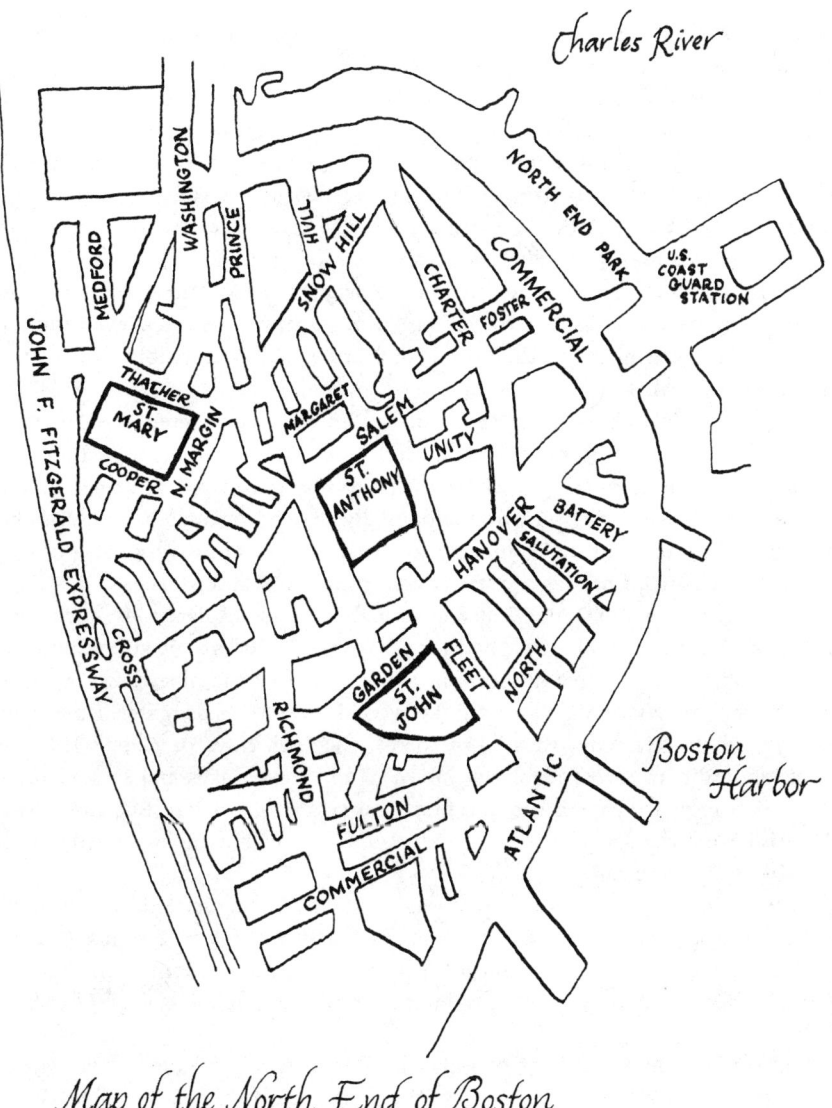

Map of the North End of Boston

has heard or read about the Old North Church on Salem Street and Paul Revere's House (both visited annually by over 100,000 tourists), but not everyone knows that the North End was the first area to be settled in the city of Boston. In the Old North Church, quiet, cool dignity prevails. The noises of traffic on Salem Street are muffled in this church whose gleaming white interior is accented with glacial gold organ pipes, fragile-looking candle-filled chandeliers and high box-pews. Paul Revere's house is a small wooden cabin-like structure located in the North Square. It is filled with silverwork, tools, furniture, and other memorabilia which demonstrate the simple way of life of our early American fathers. Tourists are also attracted to Copp's Hill, the pre-Revolutionary cemetery in which many of the pitted tombstones still bear visible signs of the British musket balls.

In pre-Revolutionary days, the North End was considered the heart of Boston. Paul Revere, John Hancock, and John Adams gathered with other patriots at Salutation and North (now Hanover) Streets for meetings of the 'North End Caucus' (the term was supposedly derived from ships' calkers who were strong in numbers and staunchly for separation from British rule). For two centuries the North End was the stronghold of the English settlers.

From 1850 to 1900 the Yankee stronghold was displaced by successive immigrant waves of Irish, Jews, and then Italians. The Irish arrived first, settling in the North End in large numbers in the first half of the nineteenth century. Back in the heyday of Major John F. Fitzgerald (he and his daughter, Rose, now Mrs. Joseph P. Kennedy, were born there), the Irish boys of Copp's Hill and those of Endicott Street regularly 'mixed it up.' Dance halls and saloons lined Hanover Street, which marked the first Irish center of Boston. But along with the Irish who were in the majority came a few Italian families, mostly from northern Italy, especially from Genoa.

During the 1870s, the North End was rapidly becoming settled by Jews from Eastern Europe and a minority of other nationalities—Poles, Russians, Greeks, and Portuguese. Salem and Hanover Streets soon became predominantly Jewish. Several synagogues were eventually built, one of them at the end of Jerusalem Place.

Until 1850 there is record of only one Jewish family residing in the North End—that of Moses Michael Hays (Weisberg 1962:1). In the early 1860s, some Jewish merchants who lived in the South End of Boston began to open stores in the North End for the sale of men's and boys' ready-made clothing, a business that was fast becoming popular in the United States. Some years later a number of Jewish families started to open stores for the buying and selling of second-hand clothing and they made their living quarters in the back of the stores. Then in the early 1870s, a few peddlers from the South End began to move to the North End in order to take advantage of the Saturday night business in the market district. Soon *minyans* (congregations) for religious purposes were organized and there began to emerge the North End Jewish community, which in the next fifty years was to play a leading role in the development of Boston life.

From 1860 to 1880 the Jewish population grew rapidly, fed by the waves of immigration from Eastern Europe. The boats landing at Boston's harbors were filled with relatives and *Landsleit* of earlier arrivals already settled in the North End to whom they naturally gravitated. Most of the young men among the newcomers were in the midst of their religious studies, *yeshiva bochers*, and few of them had any skilled training. These young men were to furnish the basis for the eventual reputation of the North End as an educated community of Jews. The Russian pogroms from 1881-1884 brought mass immigration of a different type. Entire families now came. Men learned all kinds of vocational skills and became mechanics, carpenters, tailors, jewelers, and traders. They made a perfect blend with the earlier arrivals. Every home now had to crowd in an additional person or persons, no matter how few the rooms, until permanent housing could be found for these newly arrived immigrants. This mass immigration led to the development of the West End, East Boston, and Chelsea as Jewish communities, followed by Roxbury, Dorchester, and Mattapan.

With the turn of the twentieth century, a change became noticeable in the North End. Prosperity and progress were making their imprints. Success prompted the North End Jewish residents to move to finer homes in the suburbs. The once pulsating Jewish center of life and learning of the North End quickly faded away. It was during this period that a large number of Italian immigrants began to settle in the North End. Therefore it is only within the last fifty to sixty years that Italians have made their mark in this district of Boston.

By the 1920s Italians had achieved a majority and later during World War II, this ethnic group accounted for 98.0 percent of the area's peak population of 20,000. The Italians have fought long and hard to preserve a self-determined isolation for the past half-century. But the struggle of North Enders to establish their ethnic identity in their precious sanctuary-type district was quite challenging. Around the turn of the century, only a small colony of Genovese Italians lived in the North End along with people from many other ethnic groups who had migrated to the United States and settled along the Atlantic seaboard. Today the neighborhood is 89.0 percent Italian. Within this Italian-American community, there is one large segment which wants desperately to maintain the status quo; it resents incursions by outsiders. The other group which is smaller and younger in age, far from being alarmed, welcomes the dwindling Italian control and looks upon it as healthy for the area.

Many Italians—Tuscans, Sicilians, Romans, Neopolitans, Calabrese, Abruzzese, and Genovese—have all come to the United States with the idea that one day when they, like their *paisani* before them, have had their share in American opportunity and prosperity, they would then return to their beloved homeland with their wealth to enjoy their remaining days. Believing that the streets in America were 'glittering with gold,' they discovered the grim reality that city life in America was gutters, unpaved streets, sidewalks, and walk-up tenements. Many disillusioned immigrants were disappointed to find that work in the factory was not readily available to them, because in many cases they were skilled farm workers and they lacked the necessary skills for American industry.

Although immigrants have always faced countless hardships in becoming acculturated to the American way of life, the hard fact is that the vast majority of these immigrants have never returned permanently to Italy. The half dozen travel agents in the North End who handle much of the trans-Atlantic travel arrangements for this Italian-American community agree that although North Enders take advantage of the popular summer vacation packaged trips to Italy in order to visit their relatives and friends, there is only a handful of families who choose to return and live permanently in their native Italy. Once exposed to the opportunities offered in America, and once having minimally overcome language barriers, these immigrants are no longer attracted by the thought of returning to their villages, towns, or cities. This is particularly true when there are no longer any family ties back in Italy.

The most recent immigrants to the North End in the late 1960s and early 1970s acclimate fairly quickly to their new surroundings for a number of reasons: the similarity in the quality of the food; church services in the Italian language; the social solidarity found within the fraternal club (*società*); and the familiarity of the various Italian dialects. But perhaps the most visible reason for a smoother transition is the modernization and higher quality of life which have made their own impact on Italians in Italy. The period of transition from an all encompassing Italian culture to a predominant American culture has become of shorter duration due to a great deal of americanization of present-day Italian life-styles. The newly arriving immigrants have become accustomed to American culture with fewer emotional, linguistic, and social anxieties than previous generations of Italian immigrants.

Housing

Despite new storefronts along the North End's main artery of Hanover Street, the exterior of the neighborhood is quite old in marked contrast to many remodeled interior apartments. The majority of the buildings surrounded by the waterfront and the 'Hanover Iron Curtain,' as some residents have dubbed the Central Expressway, date almost exclusively from the late nineteenth century. The North End Library, Post Office, and the First District Police Station are some of the few exceptions. The North End continues to have no movie theaters, pawn shops, hotels, motels, or boarding houses. This area has remained a close-knit, tradition-bound, and self-enclosed world of approximately 3,500 families. And all present indications point to a determined effort to keep it that way.

The 12,000 North Enders live in great brick tenements, jammed together four to five stories high, dark, dirty, ancient-looking, with somewhat run-down exteriors. Although a new facade of aluminum window frames and polished blond walnut front doors often attempts to detract from the age of many of these century-old structures, visitors cannot but observe the marriage of American and foreign architecture: baroque wrought-iron fire escapes have been added onto early nineteenth century American-designed four-story tenement buildings. Flower boxes with assorted blooming flowers and herbs add color to these drab window sills and fire escapes.

The center of the North End is filled with a maze of tiny, intertwining concrete and cobblestone streets and alleys bearing the names they held in colonial times: Prince, Charter, Snow Hill, Salutation, and Salem. These twisting little ways may have been wide enough in the eighteenth century for the Bostonian's horse and carriage, but not for today's Italian-Americans with their Lincoln Continentals, Cadillacs, or Pontiacs, which are often parked jauntily on the sidewalks.

There are patios on the rooftops of many tenements where clothes are hung to dry, sunbathers soak up the summer sun, and old men successfully cultivate tomato gardens, an occasional lemon or fig tree, perhaps even some mint, basil, and oregano amid a forest of television antennas. Clotheslines are strung from fire escape to fire escape and the amount of a family's weekly linen is a reliable indicator of the number of family members.

Below on the streets lined with parked cars are scattered garbage and leftovers from peddlers and pushcart vendors. A fourth grade girl at St. Mary's Grammar School observed: 'The North End can be a pretty place to live if only people kept it clean. The streets are always dirty, full of junk. They're not cleaned up as often as they should. There are no litter baskets anywhere. I'm not ashamed to live in the North End; I'm only ashamed when the streets are dirty.'

Although residents live in close quarters in tenement buildings which touch one another, neither the noise, traffic congestion, lack of greenery, nor the refuse which fills the streets apparently irritates them. North Enders seem to take all of this hustle and bustle in stride for this is precisely what makes the North End the North End. But the same residents have become irritated in recent years; they are now balking at the soaring rents of their apartments. Some apartments rent for $150.00 to $200.00 for three rooms and as high as $300.00 for apartments with two or three bedrooms. These high rents have become commonplace for North Enders who once enjoyed the lowest rates in all of Boston. Because the majority of North End families are working-class people, many do not have sufficient means to pay for continually rising rents. Some families have decided not to pay such exorbitant rents and have moved consequently to lower rent districts of East Boston, Revere, Charlestown, Evrette, Somerville, and Dorchester; while more resourceful families have decided to purchase a mortgaged home or even rent an apartment in Newton, Brighton, Milton, Watertown, or Medford, which is quickly becoming a second North End. Commenting on the high rents in the North End, the pastor of St. Mary's Church, the Reverend Frederick Bailey, S.J., points out that resident landlords or absentee speculators believe their high rents are justified because of the present spiralling costs of high-risk fire insurance for such old buildings, ever-rising real estate taxes and costs for maintenance, utilities, and services for tenements.

Down on Commercial Street is the waterfront which some older North Enders disdainfully refer to as the 'other one-half neighborhood.' Here at one time stood factories, fruit and produce warehouses, and fisheries that were then the North End's primary source of revenue. But now the Boston Redevelopment Authority has taken over these properties and has financed redevelopment for future office buildings, luxury apartments, restaurants and shops. Many North Enders seem uneasy about this planned redevelopment area because they feel threatened by the uncertainties which this redevelopment project will bring to their own businesses, housing, and life-styles.

Churches, Schools, and Community Action Programs

There are five churches in the North End; four are Roman Catholic and the fifth is the very famous Protestant church, Christ Church, better known as the Old North Church.

St. Mary's Church on Cooper Street was founded in 1834. It is the oldest Catholic church in the North End. The Jesuit Fathers serve the Italian-American community. Two priests, the Reverend Matthew Donovan, S.J., and the Reverend Edmond Wolff, S.J., have been at St. Mary's Church since the Irish-American settlement began to move out of the North End. Because of overburdening financial difficulties for its continued operation as an elementary school, St. Mary's Grammar School closed its doors on June 22, 1973.

St. Leonard of Port Maurice Church (1873) is a Franciscan church on North Bennet Street. The Franciscan priests and brothers also administer Christopher Columbus High School for Boys which adjoins the church. St. Anthony is the grade school under the jurisdiction of St. Leonard's. St. Anthony's is the largest of all the parochial and non-parochial grade schools in the area.

Sacred Heart Church was founded by the first Genovese settlers of Boston in 1889. The Scalabrini Fathers, whose apostolic work was originally to administer to the spiritual and physical needs of newly arriving Italian immigrants, continue to be of service to many Italian-American families in the North Square area of the North End. St. John's Grammar School is under the jurisdiction of Sacred Heart Church.

The fourth Catholic Church in the area is St. Stephen's, an historic building designed in 1802 by Charles Bulfinch, one of the great early American architects. St. Stephen's was originally built as a Protestant Church to administer to the needs of the congregation that had in 1712 gathered from the overcrowded Old North Church parish. In 1843, St. Stephen's was purchased by the Boston Catholic Archdiocese and it remains the only standing Bulfinch church in all of Boston. Each of these four churches serves its parishioners, both its loyal residents and its outside, non-North End parishioners who return 'home' each Sunday to worship in the church of their youth.

Of the three high schools, two are parochial: Christopher Columbus (boys) and Julie Billart (girls). The remaining school, Michelangelo, is a junior high public school for both boys and girls in grades seven, eight, nine, and ten. Of the four grade schools, the only public school is the Eliot, which is the oldest grammar school in the United States, having been founded in 1713. The Eliot holds classes from kindergarten through the sixth grade. Children then have to transfer to Michelangelo Junior High School to continue their education.

The 1905 graduation class program of the Eliot Grammar School indicates that only fourteen out of forty-seven graduates were of Italian parentage. The majority were of Jewish extraction. Today it is quite different. The 1975 graduation class program shows that twenty-six out of thirty-three graduating students are Italian-American while the remaining seven students are of Irish and Hispanic backgrounds.

The North End is rich in community action programs, which include the famous old North Bennet Street Industrial School, which offers everything from full-time vocational training to avocational classes, from a nursery school to a gym as well as summer camp programs for the youngsters.

There are many other community agencies at work to benefit the residents: the North End Union which organized the first supervised playground in this country; the Christopher Columbus Youth Center which sponsors social, cultural, educational, and athletic activities for teenagers; the North End School Center which offers classes and group activities in many crafts.

The North End Community Action has been federally funded and has developed programs like Head Start, an employment counseling center for newly arrived immigrants, a health clinic, a legal aid office, a tenant/landlord advisory board, and at least another half dozen service-oriented agencies. The leadership role in the majority of these community agencies is carried out by former residents of the North End who now live in other sections of the city or in Boston's many suburbs. However, these men and women who guide and direct various community programs rely considerably on a handful of assistants who are residents of the North End. These assistants hold associate positions in each community program and have the important task of sifting the many problems coming from various sectors within the North End community so that appropriate action to solve the problems can be taken.

The close ties of the North End with the sea become obvious not only because of the seafood restaurants that dot the wharf area on Commercial Street, but most especially because of its residential location near the harbor. There are three seamen's houses here. The Mariner's House is located two doors away from Paul Revere's House in North Square across the street from Sacred Heart Church. It is a house open for any American seamen waiting for ships coming to Boston. The Sailor's Clubhouse on Hanover Street is operated by a fraternal organization called the Seamen's Friend Society. The United States Coast Guard Base on Commercial Street accommodates hundreds of men and vessels that service the United States' North Atlantic seacoast.

Market and Restaurants

Fridays and Saturdays are hectic days in the North End because they are market days. Thousands of shoppers of all ages, sexes, and races, rich and poor alike, come to the Italian market to carry home their week's supply of fresh vegetables and fruits, meat and fish. Students from Cambridge and residents from Beacon Hill and Boston's suburbs flock to the North End market and take home knapsacks and shopping bags brimming with groceries. Just under the viaduct at the expressway near the Government Center Public Parking Garage is Blackstone Street. On Saturdays, traffic to Blackstone Street is re-routed and this street becomes an open-air market with rows and rows of pushcarts filled with pyramid-shaped assortments of fruits and vegetables. Most of these open-market vendors are North End men and boys who have learned to discriminate North Enders from non-North End residents; they will often charge the latter a few more cents for the same quantity and quality of produce. But anyone who obviously does not look like an Italian-American but who attempts to speak Italian to the vendor will receive at least an appreciative smile if not some extra grapes, radishes, or potatoes.

Just a minute's walk from the open market on Blackstone Street (walk under the Central Expressway toward the North End proper) is Salem Street which runs perpendicular to the expressway. Salem Street begins here, at the 'Iron Curtain,' and snakes its way toward the Boston Harbor. Salem Street is the 'Market Street' of the North End. It is known all over Greater Boston for its butcher, poultry, and seafood stores besides its bakeries, pastry, and Italian imported grocery stores.

Butcher shops display in their windows white porcelain trays filled with every conceivable animal part and organ undignified with Saran Wrap: a detached head of lamb, its hide neatly removed but its eyes staring at a potential customer; kidneys, livers, tails, shin bones, cow brains and tongue, and hooves. Above these trays are large suspended meat hooks embedded in the ceiling of the butcher shop. And from these meat hooks black and white goats hang upside down. Skinned and unskinned silky furred rabbits brought down from Maine before dawn that day hang limply alongside carcasses of lambs and a variety of other marbled haunches of meat. Loops of sausage are piled high in a corner of the butcher's window. Tourists are amazed at the variety of cuts of meat and other animal parts for sale. Many wonder how they will be used in preparation for an Italian dinner.

Thick sawdust covers the floors of the two or three seafood shops on Salem Street. Sitting on layers and layers of crushed ice are codfish, squid, octopus, shrimp, and live lobster crawling slowly around nowhere. Shopkeepers assure their customers of having only freshly caught fish—caught early that very morning, or at most, no later than yesterday. In front of the seafood stores are washtubs filled with clams, oysters, crabs, quohogs, and even translucent little snails in striped brown shells crawling up the sides of the aluminum washtubs.

Grocery stores sell everything familiar to Italian tastes: rows of imported prosciutto hams, salamis, and capacolo, wrapped in the cellophaned red, white, and green Italian colors, hang alongside wax-colored, fat rounds of Provalone and Mozarella cheese. Half a dozen name brands of Tuscan olive oil and tomato pastes line the shelves. In neat, tightly packed rows in front of the stores, there are crocks of green and black wrinkled (purple pinched) olives; baskets of pale bay leaves and long-stemmed oregano; barrels of dried, salted codfish; vats of salted lupini beans; and strings of garlic bulbs and bright red and yellow peppers.

Pastry shop windows are stacked with creatively sculptured multi-tiered wedding cakes; *biscotti* (cookies) of all shapes and flavors; cakes and pies rich in custards and liqueurs; and, of course, there are trays of long, round, and rectangular shaped loaves of oven-fresh Italian bread.

The two dozen or so Italian restaurants scattered throughout this Italian quarter offer a limited number of special dishes. Some restaurants list only regional gourmet dishes like tortellini alla Lucchese, manicotti alla Bolognese, saltimbocca alla Romana, or aragosta Fra Diavolo Neapolitan style. Others offer specialized provincial home-styled cooking of ravioli, mastoccioli, hand-rolled gnocchi di patate or minestrone cooked by the husband and served by his wife at the family owned and operated restaurant like Mamma Anna's on Hanover Street. Weekend evenings invite an amalgamated breed of faithful patrons to the North End: casually dressed students from Cambridge, Chestnut Hill, and Newton; suburbanites and former North Enders returning to the old neighborhood. Friends mingle together for a leisurely multi-coursed dinner lasting several enjoyable hours.

Italian Religious Festivals

The biggest and most exciting attractions in the North End take place every weekend in July and August. It is the season of *le feste*. It is a time when streets are corded off to traffic, colored lights arch across narrow streets and alleys, and V-shaped pairs of American and Italian flags attached to the light and telephone poles flutter in the wind. Visitors, tourists, and residents of the North End all come together to celebrate an Old Italian village-style *festa*.

These summer festivals are the public celebration of various Catholic saints. Following this religious tradition with its beginnings established in the towns and villages within provinces scattered throughout Italy, many Italians who immigrated to the United States brought with them from the old country the custom of honoring their community patron saint. This tradition is now being carried on by second and third generation Italian-Americans. The North End is one of the few remaining Italian colonies in the United States which carries on this time-honored Italian custom. The saints' feasts are held every weekend in July and August; the saints who are honored are: St. Rocco, St. Joseph, St.

Anthony, St. Lucy, St. Agrippina, La Madonna della Cava, La Madonna del Carmine, and La Madonna del Soccorso.

The feast of La Madonna del Soccorso (Our Lady of Help), for example, is a carryover celebration of the days when the first immigrant Sicilian fishermen, who lived on the waterfront, had a strong devotion to the Virgin Mary. Italian fishermen of the North End have continued this long Christian tradition of dedicating themselves in a public ritual to Our Lady of Help by asking her to intercede for their safety and success while on fishing excursions in the North Atlantic waters.

Each religious festival differs in its liturgical celebration, particular street locale, and the degree of flamboyancy, but all the feasts follow the same general schedule. On Friday evening the statue of the particular saint is removed from its permanent chapel in the fraternal clubhouse, or *società*, and after a small procession through the North End streets, it is brought to rest in a temporary shrine in the middle of the street which is closed off for the festival weekend. Later that same evening, there are music and entertainment on the bandstand and dancing in the streets, followed by a firework display. On Saturday and Sunday afternoons, there is a lengthier procession with the statue of the saint throughout all the streets of the North End. After the Roma Band concert on Sunday evening, the statue is brought back to its permanent chapel.

During the Saturday and Sunday afternoon processions, husky male members from the particular religious society sponsoring the festival take turns carrying the heavy plaster statue on their shoulders. While these men carry the honored statue of the saint, other uniformed members of the *società* collect one, five, ten, and sometimes even twenty dollar bills thrown at them by residents from tenement windows and by bystanders. These bills are sometimes folded and attached by a clothespin and tossed out of a window or rooftop; but most of the time the bills are crunched into a ball and tossed at the statue. The uniformed honor guard collect these bills and pin them to the cape hanging from the saint's shoulders. Frequently at the end of the weekend festival, the saint's delicate features are barely visible beneath the overlapping streamers of dollar bills. This money is used partially to finance the festival while the remaining amount is used for the maintenance of the society's clubhouse and charities sponsored by the *società*.

During the evenings of the weekend feasts, there are many things to occupy the young and old alike. There are carnival rides, games, open-air concerts by the Roma Band, and dancing in the streets. In almost every available space on the street you can see vendors with their pushcarts selling hot sausage, pepper, or spicy meatball sandwiches; cold clams and oysters on the half-shell; pizza pies, and the usual popcorn, ice cream, and 'slush' (lemonade).

The festivals are occasions which invite former North Enders to come back home to the old neighborhood to visit relatives and to renew acquaintances. These feasts also attract many curious visitors and tourists who enjoy participating in the frivolity, openness, laughter, carefree spirit as well as the religious spirit of these Italian-Americans—a cultural ensemble of the profound with the profane.

But the festivals are not held in such high esteem by everyone, especially by a small number of younger residents. There are some second and third generation Italian-Americans who dislike them because they feel these festivals have slowly developed into an all-engrossing commercialized enterprise which is ethnically embarrassing to Italian-Americans. But the vast majority of North Enders disagree. One Sicilian man who has lived in the North End for over fifty years says: '*Grazie Dio*, we can still have this beautiful excuse for old friends and *paisani* to get together once a year—otherwise, we could only get to see each other at wakes and weddings' (Tramontozzi 1972:70).

Crime

Older North Enders are quick to make comparisons between their children's generation and that of their grandchildren. These grandparents note that their grandchildren's behavior is far more unrestricted than that of their own parents' when they themselves were growing up. The older residents cite the use of drugs, the apparent liberal use of money, and too little respect for older persons like themselves as the consequences of their grandchildren's personal and seemingly nonparentally guided and controlled behavior. But according to statistics from the Metropolitan Boston Police Department (personal communication), drug arrests of North End juveniles over the last four years have been less than one percent. Although 2,938 persons under the age of twenty-one (or 25.0 percent of the total North End population) live in the North End, this area has the second lowest juvenile delinquency rate of Boston's twenty-two urban residential sections. But the older folks continue to feel concern for their grandchildren's growing liberal attitudes and behavior; some even fear that one or another grandson is destined to eventually get into trouble with the police.

In spite of the high population density, narrow and poorly lit streets, the crime rates in the North End remain astonishingly low. The North End crime rates against person and property (per 1,000 permanent residents) are among the lowest in all of Boston's police districts.

Police District One, located in the heart of Boston, includes most of the downtown shopping and business districts, as well as such landmarks as the State House, Boston's City Hall, the Boston Common and Public Garden, and the Massachusetts General Hospital. District One is divided into five neighborhoods: (1) North End; (2) Beacon Hill-West End; (3) Government Center; (4) Downtown-South Cove; and (5) Chinatown. Most of the District's permanent residents live in the North End and the Beacon Hill-West End areas; the latter area is composed of students, secretaries, young professionals, and longtime Boston residents. A smaller number of residents live in Chinatown, located to the south of the district. No one lives in the Government Center complex.

Though District One contains only four percent of the city's residents, it accounts for approximately 10.0 percent of the serious crime reported to the Boston Police. The reasons for this are varied, but there appear to be two important factors involved. First, a very large share of Boston's daily population is made up of persons coming to work in the Downtown and Government Center areas. The city population increases from some 650,000 to over 1,300,000 persons daily. Secondly, the variety of goods and services that abound in District One not only attract businessmen, shoppers, moviegoers, and tourists, but also attract those who are interested in criminal activity. The district contains a large number of bars and lounges that attract a percentage of transients and tourists.

The statistics given by the Boston Police Department's Informational Service Office for all reported crimes from January 1, 1970 through June 30, 1974 (personal communication) indicate that serious crimes in District One are concentrated in the Downtown-South Cove area, with the Beacon Hill-West End section having the next highest number of offenses. Both the North End and Chinatown areas are relatively safe, with a low risk of being robbed on the streets or otherwise seriously victimized.

> At least statistically then, the North End appears to be a relatively safe place in which to live. Crimes against the person are quite low, while many of the crimes against property occur within that area bounded by the waterfront and Richmond and Hanover Streets. Much of the reason for the low rates of crimes lies no doubt in the strong familial controls and neighborhood ethos existing in the North End. The strong ethnic and religious identification among the majority of the residents makes the North End a community of people rather than a community of residents. (Cardarelli 1970:14).

Although only .01 percent of all Italian-Americans are involved in some kind of crime (Gambino 1973:72), there continues an undercurrent of feeling among non-North End Bostonians that extensive Mafia activity is present in the North End district. Residents who have lived in the North End for generations have become indifferent to accusations of Mafioso activity.

Gambling, however, is another matter. Gambling in the North End is not only commonly practiced by both men and women, it is also defended as a healthy form of recreation or amusement. One man said: 'What is so terrible for an old man or lady who is retired, bored, or lonely to bet an occasional half-dollar or dollar on a number or horse? It gives the person something to look forward to, something to hope for.'

Although the North End may be free statistically of crimes such as armed robbery, rape, or homicide, some residents believe the North End remains peaceful and relatively free of crime only because some Mafia-connected families reside in the area and help keep it that way to avoid as much overt and personal attention or attraction as possible. A number of North End parents, however, believe the reason for the relatively low crime rate in the North End is due to the close-knit, quasi-interfamilial relationship between the residents and shopkeepers. For example, it is a well-known fact that shopkeepers in the North End generally avoid calling in the police (thus no crimes are reported or recorded) when a North End child or teenager is caught shoplifting or vandalizing private property. Shopkeepers contact the delinquent's parents, restitution is quickly made, and due punishment is meted out to the youngster by his father. Thus a rather unique kind of social control among residents is keenly felt to be operative in the North End. Personal differences, difficulties, and even serious conflicts are often dealt with within the family-like structure of neighborhood residents and merchants without the intervention of District One's policemen.

Visitors to the area are mistaken to think that this old section of Boston is where criminals and violence lurk in every dark corner. North Enders are proud that their district is publicly recognized for its safety. One informant who has lived in the North End since 1931 recalls an incident in the mid-1950s in which some North End men, supposedly connected with the Mafia, not only carried out their own appropriate and effective policing but meted out their own form of justice as well. It seems that a number of Coast Guard servicemen were periodically being mugged and robbed as they were walking late at night through the North End on their way to the Coast Guard base at the end of Hanover Street. Before the police could establish any relevant facts about the case, certain Mafiosi made an investigation on their own. They quickly found the guilty men, a few North End hoodlums, and sent them to Massachusetts General Hospital as a result of their severe beatings. This conception of justice is rather natural to the background of Mafia members, who are suspicious of laws in general and of police corruption. Their philosophy of personal, responsible interaction is live-and-let-live which is summed up more succintly: 'You be a gentleman and I'll be a gentleman.'

Charles Falco, manager of the Little City Hall on Parmentier Street, has been an ardent supporter and leader of the North End. He becomes emotional when he talks about outsiders' preoccupation with the Mafia's supposedly entrenched organized criminal operations there.

> Never have I been interviewed by anyone—students, researchers, reporters—that the big question hasn't come up—what about the Mafia? Mafia, Mafia, Mafia all the time. I'm sick and tired of it. How many of these people realize that the Mafia that started in Italy, in Sicily, was only a political resistance group and it carried over into this country as a means of survival when Italian immigrants were discriminated against and by all the other larger ethnic groups as well? Like all good things that start out being noble, some members got carried away and violence became the 'equalizer.' Today, look at the Mayor's Crime Check survey. There is less violence and vandalism here than anywhere else in the city. (Tramontozzi 1972:60)

The Italian-American Community

The characteristics denoting the North End go beyond the North End's geographical location, referring also to history, business enterprises, or religious manifestations. The North End is essentially its people—its 12,000 permanent residents: people like the very many visible old men sitting on benches in Paul Revere Park reading the Italian-American daily newspaper, 'Il Progresso'; playing card games like *scopa, briscola*, or *tresette*; or simply puffing on their dried-out, rope-like Parodi cigars while laughing or speaking perhaps of the foibles, frenzies, and faux pas of *paisani*. Whether listening intently or yelling vigorously, these men enjoy their animated conversations with one another. There are mothers who stroll hand in hand with their children or who periodically pop their heads out of windows, shouting at their children not to make so much noise while playing street hockey, scatter, or hide-and-seek in the narrow alleys and gangways, some of which are so narrow that they are one-way passageways for people.

Wherever you go in the North End, you will see people talking with one another, on the streets, in front of shops, in parks, standing around walls and sitting on benches. From the impression given by both older and younger men milling around in the middle of the day on street corners, smoking their cigarettes or Parodi cigars, visitors are tempted to judge these Italian-American men to be simply *lazzaroni* (lazy individuals). But many of these younger or middle-aged men are newly arrived immigrants who work at night as cooks, chefs, bakers, and bartenders, while the elderly men are retired or semi-retired. But according to a marriage counselor at the *Società Catolica* in North Square, there is a growing number of young immigrant men who are jobless not because they cannot find employment, but because these men expect to find top-salaried construction positions immediately open to them. They are determined to bide their time and wait until they can get a job at their anticipated salary.

But no matter if the North End is made up of men or women or children, young or old, Boston-born or immigrant Italian, all characteristically congregate in small groups and carry on animated conversations with a great deal of gusto.

One cultural cohesive factor binding the residents together is their obvious Italian ethnic heritage of which they are continually being reminded by living in such an Italian milieu. This Italian culture is communicated, shared, and reinforced in a number of ways: by the quality of the foods eaten; the clubs, schools, and churches attended; and especially by the various dialects spoken within this community. The Italian which is spoken here is best described as a conglomeration of Southern Italian dialects which over the last forty to fifty years have incorporated numerous italianized American words. The English spoken in the North End is English that is heard nowhere else in New England or in Boston. North Enders have the strong tendency toward being uniquely apart—they are not quite Italian, but not quite American either.

But as any ethnic group set apart and defensively insular, the North End Italian-Americans have worries. Principally they share anxieties due to the encroachment of outsiders, especially housing speculators and redevelopers in the area and periodic attempts by black families to integrate within the North End community. North Enders have been distrustful of private developers and city officials who have been purchasing many of the old factories, warehouses, and vacant property lots along the waterfront on Commercial Street and then gradually converting them into remodeled, rentable offices, luxury apartments, and shops. Residents of the area also became suspicious, even hostile, toward real estate speculators who, while waiting for financial support for redevelopment, were temporarily allowing a growing number of transient and itinerant artists, writers, and dropouts to pay rent for makeshift apartments in these abandoned buildings in 'ghost town,' as the children refer to this dilapidated waterfront area.

A large number of North End adults manifest a strong racial tension and their own children reflect their prejudices against the blacks. In 1971, a black family moved into an apartment on Salem Street. Within forty-eight hours this family had moved out of this same apartment because their lives were seriously threatened. The landlord was pressured with verbal threats of violence; one threat promised that the apartment building would be blown up if the black family did not move out immediately. The black family's windows were smashed and the family car was practically destroyed by vandalism. Many of the North Enders became extremely nervous at this time when their homogeneous way of life appeared threatened by this one black family. Residents of the North End felt then and continue to feel that they have a right to be custodians of their geographical enclave. They justify their thoughts and feelings to preserve their ethnic identity and cultural heritage because, as they argue, they, their parents, and their grandparents fought long and hard to establish a voluntary, self-imposed and self-determined isolation for the past half-century. If they should lose any part of the North End, they feel they will lose a part of themselves.

This self-identification with the area has not produced all negative results, however. The very strong cooperative and communal concern for one another is a positive expression of the self-identification of this community. One North End resident exemplified this close-knit, extended family type of relationship among the residents when he referred to the apartment house fire near the Prince Street end of Salem Street one cold night in February, 1971. This fire was the largest in an erratic series of apartment house fires which had been occurring. In this particular fire, an entire city block of apartments and first-floor stores was ablaze, threatening to spread throughout the whole North End. Fortunately, not one person died in this tragedy. Residents assisted the firemen and police to control the fire and to help the stricken families. The fire victims were immediately taken in and cared for by a number of other families. On the day following the fire, a Fire Relief Fund was established through the cooperative efforts of the North End Catholic churches, Little City Hall, Knights of Columbus, and a number of the Italian fraternal societies. Within a few days the fire victims were provided with clothing, food, and funds to help them get started again. What had not been publicly known was that during the series of arson fires within the North End community, a group of residents teamed up to patrol the area twenty-four hours a day for months on end, hoping to catch the arsonist. No one was ever caught, but since the Salem Street tragedy, no major arson-type fire has broken out in the North End.

The North End community may occasionally complain about the droves of tourists and visitors, especially those who drive into the area's already heavily congested traffic, but most visitors are treated graciously and congenially in the restaurants, shops, markets, and even in the streets when asking for directions from a North Ender. Nearly a half million visitors who walk the Freedom Trail each year must walk through the North End to see some of the more interesting historical sites. The area residents do not count on the tourist trade for their livelihood, although many tourists do stop in an Italian restaurant or espresso bar.

Conclusion

In summary, the general nonverbalized ethnic principle governing the life-styles of the Italian-Americans in the North End is that they share the same day-in and day-out concerns, worries, prejudices, ideals, and goals as other ethnic communities whose immigrant relatives before them came to the United States to establish new roots in a land great with promise and opportunity. Many Old World values continue to be held in high esteem in the North End; religion continues to play an important idealized role within the family structure, at least in the formative years of the children. The Italian-American family is typically father-dominated with a characteristic strict disciplinary attitude toward the children—a mark found rather often in the majority of these families which are considered socioeconomically to be working-class type families, families in which members usually give and receive much warmth, affection, and emotional security.

3
Variable Analysis of Interdental Fricatives

General Remarks

One of the most significant contributions of sociolinguistics in the last decade has probably been the insight that various social dialects in the United States are not differentiated from one another by discrete sets of linguistic features, but by the variations in the frequency with which certain linguistic features occur. As is described in Chapter 1, various studies of social dialects in the United States in the mid and late 1960s have clearly demonstrated that dialects could no longer be effectively and precisely differentiated by simple, categorical statements but rather require more generalized, quantitative criteria. It was also discovered that many instances of fluctuation in the use of socially diagnostic linguistic features were found to be characterized by inherent variability rather than dialect borrowing, mixture, or leveling. Labov's classic study (1966), Shuy, Wolfram, and Riley's sociolinguistic study of Detroit Black English (1968), as well as Labov and associates' analysis of Black English in New York City (1968), Wolfram's study of sociolinguistic differences in Detroit's Black English (1969), and finally Fasold's description of black working-class speech in Washington, D.C. (1972), all indicate the absolute requirement of including the concept of variability in the study of social dialects in the United States. One of the many rewarding results of these sociolinguistic studies has been the growing recognition on the part of many linguists that inherent variability must somehow be taken into account whenever linguistic phenomena are analyzed.

The above-mentioned sociolinguistic studies have all demonstrated that there are both independent linguistic constraints such as phonological and syntactical environments and nonlinguistic constraints such as age, sex, education, ethnicity, and socioeconomic class, which directly and immediately affect the variable usage of various linguistic features. There has been a slow but steadily growing enthusiasm and support by many linguists for the view that variable constraints might be formally included in a representative linguistic variable rule.

The present study of American English spoken by Italian-American children in Boston's North End demonstrates the presence of systematic variability in the usage of certain linguistic features which are presented in the following chapters: Chapter 4 discusses word-final consonant cluster simplification while Chapter 5 analyzes third person singular present tense verb concord. Here in Chapter 3, a variable analysis of both voiced and voiceless interdental fricatives //d// and //θ// is presented. This analysis is modeled on similar methodological procedures used in many other sociolinguistic studies of social dialects, especially in Wolfram (1969, 1974) and in Fasold (1972).

The //d// and //θ// variables. According to Wolfram (1974:66), the most widely recognized phonological indicators of social status in American English are the interdental fricatives, //d// and //θ//, both of which are represented orthographically by the letters *th*. The variants of interdental fricatives are shared by many nonstandard varieties of American English including the English speakers in the North End of Boston. In order to view the different dimensions of these variables and the manner in which they pattern, it is necessary to analyze each variable in terms of its different positional occurrences, namely, in word-initial, medial, and final positions.

At the beginning of a word such as *them*, *th-* is frequently pronounced as a voiced apico-alveolar stop //d// in casual speech of Italian-American children in the North End. Consequently, such words as *them, these*, and *that* are pronounced as *dem, dese*, and *dat* respectively. Although other children in all parts of the United States, who could be considered Standard English speakers, will sometimes pronounce in casual or informal speech the voiced apico-alveolar stop //d// for the voiced interdental fricative //d//, North End children pronounce initial *th-* as //d// with far greater regularity. In using variable //d//, North End children are very much like Black English speaking children of New York City (Labov 1966, 1972b) and Detroit (Wolfram 1969) who have been known to pronounce *this, these, than* and similar words with the voiced apico-alveolar stop in a systematic manner.

In the case of voiceless interdental fricative //θ//, the *th-* in initial position in such words as *think, thank*, and *thin* is pronounced by the Italian-American children as the variable voiceless apico-alveolar stop //t//. *Think, thank*, and *thin* are pronounced consequently as *tink, tank*, and *tin* respectively.

Within a word, the voiced interdental fricative is also variably pronounced as the voiced apico-alveolar stop. For example, *mother, although*, and *another* are pronounced by the North End children as *moder, all-dough*, and *anoder*, respectively. The voiceless *-th-* appearing in medial position in *anything, Anthony*, and *bathroom* is generally pronounced not as //θ// but rather as //t//, which results in *anyting, Antony*, and *batroom*.

The voiced interdental fricative //d// also appears in word-final position as in *bathe, clothe, lathe*, and *soothe*. In examining all recorded data of all sixty informants, only two words exemplifying a potential voiced interdental fricative in final position were found: *smooth* and *breathe*. These two words, each spoken by different informants, were pronounced with variable //d// as in *smood* and *breed*. No other examples of word-final voiced interdental fricative were noted. However, the data revealed an abundance of examples of words ending in voiceless *-th* as in *with, North, both*, and *fourth* which are variably pronounced as *wit, nort, boat*, and *fort*, respectively, by the North End children.

3 Variable analysis of third person singular present tense verb concord / 41

Word-initial Voiced *th-*

Before examining word-initial voiced *th-* in greater detail, it is first necessary to describe briefly the procedures used in extracting and tabulating the data for word-initial voiced *th-*. All examples of potential word-initial voiced *th-* were taken exclusively from the spontaneous conversation sections of the interviews with each of the sixty informants, but no more than ten examples of word-initial voiced *th-* were taken from any informant. Moreover, identical words beginning with voiced *th-* were collected no more than two times for any informant. For example, although the word *them* might be extracted from only two different loci in casual speech and tabulated a maximum number of two times for any informant, *them* could have occurred far more frequently in an informant's recorded spontaneous conversation.[1] Each example of word-initial voiced *th-* was then transcribed phonetically on an index card. The methodology used to extract and represent the data for easy retrieval has been already described in Chapter 1.

The number of examples of words beginning with potential //ð// which were extracted from all sixty informants totalled 574. Of this number, ninety words (or 15.7 percent) were clearly pronounced with the standard voiced interdental fricative //ð//, while 484 examples (or 84.3 percent) were clearly pronounced with the socially stigmatized variant voiced apico-alveolar stop //d//. The frequency of word-initial voiced *th-* in both its standard and nonstandard realizations are given in Table 3.1.

Table 3.1. Comparison in the use of standard and nonstandard features for word-initial voiced *th-* in the speech of the North End Italian-American children

	Standard feature //ð//	Nonstandard feature //d//
Number of examples	90	484
Percent of usage	15.7	84.3
N = 574		

Constraints for word-initial voiced th-. Two types of preceding environmental constraints on the incidence of //d// were examined. First, it was hypothesized that a preceding consonant might increase the incidence of //d// as opposed to a preceding vowel. Table 3.2 gives the figures for the despirantized form of the voiced apico-alveolar stop when it was preceded by a consonant and by a vowel. From the statistical analysis shown in Table 3.2, we see that the hypothesis that the preceding consonant favors despirantization more than a preceding vowel is not substantiated; that is, no variable constraint is apparently based on whether

Table 3.2. Comparison of the effect of a preceding consonant or vowel on word-initial voiced *th*-

	C## __	V## __
Intact	54	26
Despirantized	357	137
Percent despirantized	86.9	84.6
N = 574		

or not the preceding segment is a consonant. The analysis of the empirical data in Table 3.2 clearly demonstrates that the percentages of despirantization for preceding consonants and preceding vowels are so close in range of frequency, 86.9 percent and 84.6 percent, that it becomes almost impossible to judge definitively that either a preceding consonant or a preceding vowel is the true constraint. However, when the preceding consonants were further analyzed and distinguished on the basis of voicing, there appeared a discernible constraint. Table 3.3 clearly indicates that there is a higher frequency of //d// when the preceding consonants were voiceless rather than voiced. Therefore, the effect of preceding voiceless consonants, 93.1 percent, seems to indicate that the voiced apico-alveolar stop is favored more often than the voiced interdental fricative for word-initial voiced *th*-.

Table 3.3. Comparison of the effect of preceding voiced and voiceless consonants on word-initial voiced *th*-

	Voiced C##__	Voiceless C##__
Intact	44	10
Despirantized	222	135
Percent despirantized	83.5	93.1
N = 411		
$X^2 = 6.82$ $p < .01$		

A second type of analysis was performed on all 574 examples of voiced *th*-. The phonological environment immediately following voiced *th*- was carefully studied. It was found that without exception a vowel immediately follows *th*-. It was then hypothesized that the particular quality of the vowel present after word-initial voiced *th*- would favor the presence or absence of the standard form //d//. When all 574 examples were examined with regard to the vowel quality appearing immediately after voiced *th*-, it was found that all high vowels, as in *this* and *these*, favored the nonstandard //d// form as Table 3.4 shows.

Table 3.4. Comparison of the effect of high vowels and non-high vowels on word-initial voiced *th*-

	High vowels	Nonhigh vowels
Intact	3	87
Despirantized	62	422
Percent despirantized	95.4	82.9

N = 574
$X^2 = 5.87$ $p < .05$

The application of the Chi-square test of statistical significance for high and nonhigh vowel environments among the Italian-American children indicates that this distinction is significant, at the .05 level of confidence. Most clear-cut constraints on variability show a higher confidence level.

When the preceding potential constraints of voiced and voiceless consonants were compared to the following potential constraints of high and nonhigh vowels, the percentages of all the potential constraints became clearly discernible, as Table 3.5 shows.

Determining the hierarchy of constraints. It now remains to determine the hierarchy of constraints regarding word-initial voiced *th*-. One method to determine the hierarchy of variable constraints is to tabulate the cross products of the potential constraints. All four potential constraints for voiced *th*- were categorized in pairs as is shown in Table 3.5.

Table 3.5. Cross products of potential constraints on word-initial voiced *th*-

Constraints		No. despirantized/ No. observed	Percent despirantized
Voiceless C ##	High vowel	36/36	100.0
Voiceless C ##	Nonhigh vowel	149/166	89.8
Voiced C ##	High vowel	26/29	89.7
Voiced C ##	Nonhigh vowel	273/343	79.6

From Table 3.5, we can see that two potential constraints seem to be operating on despirantization of initial voiced *th*-: whether the final segment of the preceding word is a voiced or voiceless consonant, and whether the following vowel is high or nonhigh. Note that the highest percentage of despirantization occurs when a word ending with a voiceless consonant precedes word-initial *th*- and when *th*- is followed by a high vowel. The lowest percentage of despirantization occurs when the preceding word ends with a voiced consonant and when the following segment is a nonhigh vowel. This suggests that a voiceless consonant preceding *th*- favors its despirantization while a voiced consonant preceding *th*- inhibits this phenomenon. Therefore, a preceding voiceless consonant is a constraint favoring despirantization of word-initial voiced *th*-. Furthermore, the quality of the vowel following *th*- also has an effect on its despirantization. The presence of a high vowel appears to favor the phenomenon more often than the presence of a nonhigh vowel, so that a high vowel following *th*- appears to be another constraint. However, the hierarchy of the constraints cannot be determined with certainty with the available data since the cross products show that the percentage of despirantization is about the same when only the preceding environment is favorable (89.8 percent), in contrast to when only the following environment is favorable (89.7 percent). In other words, it is not possible to conclude from the results which of the two is more important due to the fact that for the two cases where one of the constraints is present and the other absent, the frequencies are separated by only .1 percent (89.8 percent vs. 89.7 percent). Since a minor change in the data could reverse this order (for example, if one more despirantization occurred in the Voiced C ## _____ High Vowel environment), it was judged that the constraints should be assigned the alpha weighting.

Variable rule for word-initial voiced th-. Assigning Greek letters in order of rank, the variable rule for word-initial voiced *th*- can be written as:

$$\begin{bmatrix} +\text{cons} \\ +\text{cont} \\ +\text{ant} \\ +\text{vd} \end{bmatrix} \rightarrow ([-\text{cont}]) \;/\; A\;([-\text{voice}]) \;\;\#\#\underline{\quad}A \begin{bmatrix} +\text{voc} \\ -\text{hi} \end{bmatrix}$$

Read: A word-initial voiced interdental fricative becomes variably despirantized, and this despirantization is equally favored when the preceding word ends in a voiceless consonant and when *th*- is immediately followed by a high vowel.

Word-medial Voiced -*th*-

The first ten examples of word-medial voiced -*th*-, such as *smother, neither, farther,* and *northern,* were extracted from the spontaneous conversation sections of the tape recorded interviews of all sixty Italian-American children. Identical words having voiced -*th*- in medial position were counted no more than two times for an informant. The original number of examples having voiced -*th*- in medial position totalled 439. Of this number, 325 (or 74.0 percent) were clearly pronounced with the socially stigmatized apico-alveolar stop, whereas

3 Variable analysis of third person singular present tense verb concord / 45

114 examples (or 26.0 percent) were pronounced with the standardized voiced interdental fricative, as indicated in Table 3.6.

Table 3.6. Comparison in the use of standard and nonstandard features for word-medial voiced -th- in the speech of the North End Italian-American children

	Standard feature //ð//	Nonstandard feature //d//
Number of examples	114	325
Percent of usage	26.0	74.0
N = 439		

Note that the distribution of //d// realization in Table 3.6 is quite straightforward; the incidence of the nonstandard variant of voiced -th- is considerably higher in rate of frequency than the standard variant.

Constraints for word-medial voiced -th-. The first type of environment to be analyzed was the environment immediately preceding -th-. It was found that of the eighty-six examples of word-medial -th- in which the segment immediately preceding the -th- was only a vowel as in *other* and *either*, seventy-three examples (or 84.9 percent) were pronounced with the socially stigmatized apico-alveolar stop. Of the 353 examples of word-medial -th- in which the segment immediately preceding the -th- was a consonant plus a vowel, such as in *rather, bother*, and *father*, 263 (or 74.7 percent) were also pronounced with the socially stigmatized stop. Again, there was no significant linguistic reason based on the statistical range of frequency to warrant that either the preceding consonant plus vowel or the preceding vowel alone should be seriously considered as a potential constraint.

The linguistic analysis which proved to be most rewarding, however, was the examination of the vocalic quality of all preceding vowels. In all 439 examples of word-medial -th-, each vowel preceding -th- was studied in relation to the frequency of both the despirantized voiced stop and the standard interdental voiced fricative. The results of the analysis strongly suggested that the presence of a schwa vowel [ə] in the environment immediately preceding word-medial -th- favored despirantized //d// compared to other vowels.

Of all potential word-medial -th- examples found in the spontaneous conversations of the Italian-American children, there were five words which exemplified the schwa vowel sound with the despirantization frequency rate of 81.0 percent (or 230/284); they were: *other, another, brother, mother*, and *smother*. The remaining eight words representing nonschwa vowel sounds with the despirantization rate of 56.5 percent (or 78/138) were: *bother, father, farther, rather, together, either, neither,* and *northern.*

It is essential to note that there were also seventeen examples of three compound words: *grandmother* (occurring eight times), *grandfather* (occurring eight times), and *godfather* (occurring only once). The frequency rate of despirantized //d// for these seventeen examples was 100.0 percent; that is, in all seventeen occurrences of these compound examples, no Italian-American child pronounced any of the three compound nouns with the standard voiced interdental fricative. Nevertheless, all seventeen examples were excluded from all further tabulations because of the obvious differences in the stress pattern from the remaining 422 examples of word-medial *-th-*. *Grándmôther, grándfâther,* and *gódfâther* all have secondary stress on the vowel immediately preceding *-th-*. Table 3.7 shows the effect of the schwa vowel and nonschwa vowels on the frequency rate of the despirantized nonstandard variant //d// in word-medial *-th-*.

Table 3.7. Comparison of the effect of the schwa vowel [ə] and all other vowels on word-medial *-th-*

	[ə] _____ er##	V _____ er##
Intact	54	60
Despirantized	230	78
Percent despirantized	81.0	56.5

N = 422

X^2 = 26.96   p < .001

Determining the hierarchy of constraints. As Table 3.7 indicates, there is only one constraint favoring despirantization for word-medial voiced *th-*. This primary constraint is the presence of a schwa vowel as the segment preceding *-th-*. Note that a higher percentage of despirantization occurs when *-th-* is preceded by a schwa (81.0 percent) than when *-th-* is preceded by any other vowel (56.5 percent). Therefore, the constellation of features specifying a schwa is assigned the alpha weighting in the variable rule given below. Furthermore, another phonological feature in the environment of the *-th-* makes the rule of despirantization apply in every instance, namely, when *-th-* occurs in compound words (e.g. *grándmôther*) which cause the vowel preceding *-th-* to become unaccented. The absence of a primary stress on the preceding vowel has a 'knockout' effect (symbolized in the variable rules as *); that is, whenever the vowel preceding *-th-* is unstressed, word-medial voiced *-th-* is categorically (i.e. 100.0 percent) despirantized independent of the effect of any other constraint in the environments.

Variable rule for word-medial voiced -th-. Thus, the variable rule for word-medial voiced -th- can be written as:

$$\begin{bmatrix} +\text{cons} \\ +\text{cont} \\ +\text{ant} \\ +\text{vd} \end{bmatrix} \rightarrow ([-\text{cont}])/ \begin{bmatrix} +\text{voc} \\ *(\sim[+\text{acc}]) \\ A\begin{pmatrix} -\text{lo} \\ +\text{back} \\ -\text{round} \\ -\text{tense} \end{pmatrix} \end{bmatrix} \underline{\qquad} [+\text{voc}]$$

Read: The despirantization of an intervocalic voiced interdental fricative is favored when the preceding vowel is schwa. It is always despirantized when the preceding vowel is unaccented.

Word-initial Voiceless *th*-

A maximum number of ten examples of the voiceless interdental fricative in initial position was culled from each informant. Although not every informant exhibited ten examples during his or her spontaneous and casual conversation, the majority of the Italian-American children did so. Of the ten examples of voiceless *th*- collected from each informant, no identical word was counted more than three times. The number three was chosen arbitrarily yet decidedly because the pilot study showed that voiceless *th*- in word-initial position was quantitatively lower in frequency of occurrence than voiced *th*- in initial position, which we have seen occurs in high frequency words such as *the*, *them*, *then*, *there*, and so on.

In his study of the social stratification of English in New York City (1966), Labov demonstrated that one of the stable sociolinguistic variables for the New York City community as a whole was the word-initial voiceless interdental fricative. Labov found that the types of variants for voiceless *th*- which can be identified tend to be common to several different nonstandard types of American English. Wolfram also discovered in his study of the overlapping influence in the English of second generation Puerto Rican teenagers in New York's Harlem (1974) that word-initial voiceless *th*- has several phonetic variant realizations: an interdental affricate [tθ] ; an unaspirated (generally lenis) stop [t] ; an aspirated stop [t] ; an apico-alveolar sibilant [s] ; and finally, no phonetic realization ∅. In studying the speech of the North End Italian-American children, the only nonstandard variant for potential voiceless *th* was //t//. The aspiration of [t] proved to be nonrelevant in the analysis of the phonetic realization of voiceless *th* in initial, medial, and final positions. Therefore, //t// was found to be the only socially stigmatized variant of voiceless *th* in the speech of the Italian-American children.

One of the principal tasks in studying the variable realization of voiceless interdental fricatives was to analyze each of the three positional occurrences of voiceless *th* in terms of their immediate preceding and following environments. Once again, it was hypothesized that it makes good linguistic sense that variability of voiceless *th* was governed by phonological constraints in the immediate preceding and following environments. The hypothesis was verified as correct by the data.

The number of examples where potential voiceless *th-* in initial position occurred totalled 635. Of this number, 85 words (or 13.4 percent) were clearly pronounced with the standard voiceless interdental fricative, whereas 550 words (or 86.6 percent) of all potential word-initial voiceless *th-* were clearly despirantized with the stigmatized voiceless apico-alveolar stop //t// as Table 3.8 shows.

Table 3.8. Comparison in the use of standard and nonstandard features for word-initial voiceless *th-* in the speech of the North End Italian-American children

	Standard feature //θ//	Nonstandard feature //t//
Number of examples	85	550
Percent of usage	13.4	86.6
N = 635		

The preceding environment for word-initial voiceless *th-* was looked into with the goal of determining whether preceding vowels or consonants had a greater effect in promoting the variable use of nonstandard //t//. The data revealed that when vowels preceded word boundary plus word-initial *th-*, the nonstandard //t// variant was used 89.3 percent (or 351/393), whereas when consonants preceded word boundary plus word-initial *th-*, the nonstandard variant //t// was used 82.2 percent (or 199/242). These statistics, however, were not judged to be highly significant in light of further analysis of the preceding consonants. When the preceding consonants were further investigated, it was found that the phonological feature of continuance played an essential role in the variability of word-initial voiceless *th-*. All the preceding consonants were carefully examined in terms of being −continuant or +continuant. Table 3.9 indicates that the number of consonants which were −continuant tended to favor, and the consonants which were +continuant tended to disfavor the despirantized variant //t// in the pronunciation of the Italian-American children.

The environment which immediately followed word-initial voiceless *th-* consisted of either a vowel plus a consonant, as in *think, thought*, and *thick*, or the consonant of a voiced retroflex [r] plus a vowel, as in *three, throw*, and *threw*. The analysis of those *th-* examples having a vowel plus a consonant after *th-* demanded that the consonants be further distinguished into obstruents and sonorants. Table 3.9 differentiates the preceding and following environments for

3 Variable analysis of third person singular present tense verb concord / 49

word-initial *th-* and gives the figures for the number of occurrences as well as the number of despirantizations and their respective percentages.

Table 3.9. Cross products of potential constraints on word-initial voiceless *th-*

Constraints	No. despirantized/ No. observed	Percent despirantized
V##___Vobs	23/24	95.8
+cons -cnt##___Vobs	10/11	90.9
V##___Vson	244/273	89.4
+cons -cnt##___Vson	102/115	88.7
V##___rV	84/96	87.5
+cons -cnt##___rV	52/63	82.5
+cons +cnt##___Vobs	2/2	*100.0
+cons +cnt##___Vson	20/29	69.0
+cons +cnt##___rV	13/22	59.1

Determining the hierarchy of constraints. Table 3.9 indicates that the higher percentages of despirantization occur when a nonstrident segment precedes voiceless *th-*. The four highest percentages occur when a nonstrident segment precedes *th-* and when a consonant follows the vocalic segment after *th-*. The lowest percentage occurs when a continuant precedes *th-* and when a vowel follows the vocalic segment [r] after voiceless *th-*. Therefore, a preceding nonstrident segment and a following consonant appear to be constraints following despirantization. Since the percentage of despirantization is higher when a nonstrident segment in the preceding environment occurs as the only favoring constraint (82.5 percent) than when the following consonant occurs alone as the favoring constraint (69.0 percent), it is suggested that the most important constraint is the preceding nonstrident segment. The second most important constraint is the following consonant. Within this latter constraint, we note that there is more despirantization when the following consonant is not a sonorant than when it is a sonorant, and therefore, the third most important constraint is a following nonsonorant consonant. Furthermore, since within the preceding nonstrident segment category, a preceding nonconsonantal segment will favor despirantization more than a consonantal segment, this makes the fourth highest constraint in the heirarchy a vowel. Note that there is one percentage (100.0 percent) which is out of order within the heirarchy. Since there were only two instances of this particular environment, it was judged that this deviantly ranked percentage should be excused on the basis of the paucity of examples found in the data.

Variable rule for word-initial voiceless th-. Thus once the Greek capital letters are assigned their respective hierarchically ranked linguistic feature weights, the variable rule can be written as:

$$\begin{bmatrix} +\text{cons} \\ +\text{cont} \\ +\text{ant} \\ -\text{vd} \end{bmatrix} \rightarrow ([-\text{cont}])/ \begin{bmatrix} A & (-\text{strid}) \\ \Delta & (-\text{cons}) \end{bmatrix} \#\# \underline{\hspace{1em}} \left(\begin{bmatrix} +\text{voc} \\ +\text{cons} \\ -\text{ant} \end{bmatrix} \begin{bmatrix} +\text{voc} \\ -\text{cons} \end{bmatrix} B \begin{bmatrix} +\text{cons} \\ \Gamma & (-\text{son}) \end{bmatrix} \right)$$

> Read: A word-initial voiceless interdental fricative becomes variably despirantized in the environment of four hierarchically ranked constraints: the most highly favoring constraint is when the preceding segment is nonstrident; the second most favoring constraint is when *th-* is followed by a consonant; the third most favoring constraint is when the following consonant is nonsonorant; and the fourth most favoring constraint is the presence of a preceding nonconsonantal segment.

Word-medial Voiceless *-th-*

There was no limit on the number of examples of word-medial voiceless *-th-* culled from the spontaneous conversations of all the Italian-American children, but again, no identical word was counted more than twice. After all examples of word-medial voiceless *-th-* were examined for both the standard and nonstandard realizations, it was found that there was a total of 271 examples of word-medial voiceless *-th-*, of which 240 (or 88.6 percent) were clearly pronounced with nonstandard //t// while only thirty-one examples (or 11.1 percent) were pronounced with the standard realization //θ//. The analysis also indicated that the majority of 271 examples of word-medial voiceless *-th-* were of a compound type; that is, there were many compound nouns in which the voiceless *th* was in reality either the final segment of a word such as *bath* as in the compound noun, *bathroom*, or was the initial segment as in *thing* of the second part of the compound as in *anything, everything, nothing,* and *something*. Consequently, word-medial voiceless *-th-* words which were compounded with two free morphemes have been separated, tabulated, and considered either as word-initial voiceless *th-* as in *(any)thing, (some)thing,* and *(every)thing* or as word-final voiceless *-th* as in *faith(ful), birth(day),* and *path(ways)*. Therefore, of the 635 examples of word-initial voiceless *th-* in Table 3.8, 162 examples were originally extracted from the tape recorded conversations as word-medial voiceless *-th-*. Of these 162 examples, 145 (or 89.5 percent) were despirantized as nonstandard //t//. In Table 3.12, of the 362 examples for word-final voiceless *-th*, thirty-one

3 Variable analysis of third person singular present tense verb concord / 51

examples were originally extracted from the children's conversations as word-medial voiceless -th-. Of these thirty-one examples, twenty-nine (or 90.6 percent) were pronounced with nonstandard //t//.

Therefore, the examples of uncompounded word-medial voiceless -th- have been reduced to: *athlete, arithmetic,* and *Anthony.* When this class of word-medial voiceless -th- examples was tabulated, the number of potential medial //θ// examples totalled only fifty-six, and of this number, forty-six (or 82.1 percent) were despirantized with the socially stigmatized variant //t// whereas only ten examples (or 17.9 percent) were pronounced with the standard pronunciation of //θ// as Table 3.10 shows.

Table 3.10. Comparison in the use of standard and nonstandard features for word-medial voiceless -th- in the speech of the North End Italian-American children

	Standard feature //θ//	Nonstandard feature //t//
Number of examples	10	46
Percent of usage	17.9	82.1
N = 56		

Constraints on word-medial voiceless -th-. The preceding environments for word-medial voiceless -th- were also studied in terms of whether or not the immediate environment preceding -th- was a vowel or a consonant. There was only one example found in the North End data where -th- was immediately preceded by a consonant (*Anthony*). In the spontaneous conversations of the Italian-American children, *Anthony* appeared fifty times. There were only two examples of -th- which were preceded by a vowel: *arithmetic* (appeared three times) and *athlete* (appeared three times). Table 3.11 shows the rate of despirantization when vowels and consonants preceded -th-.

The following environments for word-medial voiceless -th- were simply a following consonant or a following vowel. The particular consonantal features following -th- did not prove relevant in the analysis of -th-. Table 3.11 gives the figures for the variable pronunciation of word-medial voiceless -th-.

Table 3.11. Cross products of potential constraints on word-medial voiceless -th-

Constraints	No. despirantized/ No. observed	Percent despirantized
V____C	6/6	100.0
C____V	40/50	80.0

Determining the hierarchy of constraints. Given the data presented in Table 3.11, it would seem that the presence of a preceding vowel and the presence of a following consonant favor the despirantization of word-medial voiceless *-th-*. However, no definite conclusions can be reached on the basis of merely six examples for the environment of a preceding vowel and a following consonant. No true discernment on the constraints, and a fortiori, on the hierarchy of constraints can be reached with such a paucity of examples. Therefore, it has been judged that due to an insufficient number of examples of word-medial voiceless *-th-*, no variable rule could be written with any significant assurance.

Word-final Voiceless *-th*

Although there was no limit in extracting word-final voiceless *-th*, the final number of examples of word-final voiceless *-th* totalled 362. Once again no identical word was counted more than two times for any informant. Of the 362 examples of *-th*, 329 (or 90.9 percent) were pronounced with nonstandard variant //t// whereas thirty-three (or 9.1 percent) were pronounced with standard //θ// as shown in Table 3.12.

Table 3.12. Comparison in the use of standard and nonstandard features for word-final voiceless *-th* in the speech of the North End Italian-American children

	Standard feature //θ//	Nonstandard feature //t//
Number of examples	33	329
Percent of usage	9.1	90.9
N = 362		

Constraints on word-final voiceless -th. When all word-final voiceless *-th* examples were examined in terms of the preceding environment, it was apparent that there were three environments which favored the use of nonstandard //t// at various frequency rates: a preceding voiced retroflex [r], preceding vowels, and preceding consonants other than [r]. Some examples of voiced retroflex [r] preceding word-final *-th* are: *fourth*, *birth*, and *north*. Table 3.13 shows that when *-th* was preceded by [r], despirantized //t// was found to occur the highest number of times. Vowels preceding *-th* had the second highest percentage, and consonants other than [r] had the third highest number of despirantized //t//.

Examination of word-final voiceless *-th* also revealed that there were three different environments which followed *-th*: consonants, vowels, and utterance pause. Again, particular consonantal features did not seem to effect variability for *-th*. Table 3.13 represents the frequency rate of despirantized //t// for the following three types of environments in relationship to the three types of preceding environments.

3 Variable analysis of third person singular present tense verb concord / 53

Table 3.13.   Cross products of potential constraints on word-final voiceless -*th*

Constraints	No. despirantized/ No. observed	Percent despirantized
R ___ # #C	36/36	100.0
R ___ # #V	35/36	97.2
R ___ # #	3/3	*100.0
V ___ # #C	165/172	95.9
V ___ # #V	40/44	90.9
V ___ # #	16/19	84.2
C ___ # #C	20/27	74.1
C ___ # #V	9/12	75.0
C ___ # #	5/13	38.5

Determining the hierarchy of constraints. The first six percentages in Table 3.13 all occur in the absence of a preceding nonvocalic segment. Within all nine hierarchically ordered constraints, the highest percentage occurs when a voiced retroflex [r] precedes word-final voiceless -*th* and the lowest percentage occurs when a consonant precedes it. Therefore, it seems that the most important or alpha constraint is when -*th* is not preceded by a nonvocalic segment. The second most important or beta constraint is when -*th* is preceded by a vowel. Within each of these constraints, you will notice that the absence of a segment (i.e., terminal pause) following -*th* produces fewer despirantizations and therefore the absence of a segmental feature favors despirantization. Thus, the absence of a segmental feature is the third most important or gamma constraint. Within the following environment, it should also be noted that a consonantal segment produces more despirantization than a vocalic segment. Therefore, the consonant is the highest or delta constraint for word-final voiceless -*th*. The slightly deviant percentage figure (marked with an asterisk) in the hierarchically ordered scale where 100.0 percent occurred (3/3) can be attributed to the paucity of examples found in the recorded spontaneous speech of the North End children.

Variable rule for word-final voiceless -*th*. The four constraints can be incorporated within the variable rule for -*th* once the Greek capital letters have been assigned to their respective linguistic weightings. The variable rule for word-final voiceless -*th* can be written as:

$$\begin{bmatrix} +\text{cons} \\ +\text{cont} \\ +\text{ant} \\ -\text{vd} \end{bmatrix} \rightarrow ([-\text{cont}]) \;/\; \begin{bmatrix} A \sim (-\text{voc}) \\ B \begin{pmatrix} +\text{voc} \\ -\text{cons} \end{pmatrix} \end{bmatrix} \underline{\qquad} \# \# \begin{bmatrix} \Gamma \sim (+\text{seg}) \\ \Delta \, (+\text{cons}) \end{bmatrix}$$

Read: A word-final voiceless interdental fricative becomes variably despirantized in the environment of four hierarchically ranked constraints: the most highly favoring constraint is when *-th* is preceded by a true consonant (i.e., not a vowel or [r]); the second most favoring constraint is when *-th* is preceded by a vowel; the third most favoring constraint is when the word ending in *-th* is not immediately followed by another word; and if a following segment is, in fact, present, then, the fourth most favoring constraint is a consonantal segment.

Correlations with Social Factors

Since the late 1960s it has been a well-known fact among some linguists that certain linguistic features correlate strongly with social factors such as age, sex, educational achievement, ethnicity, socioeconomic status, and so on. Much research has been carried out within the last ten years and an increasing number of developmental insights have pointed the way to a better understanding of the interrelationships of social factors on speech performance and on language variation (Labov 1966; Wolfram 1969, 1974; Fasold 1972). We have mentioned previously that although the sixty North End informants come from socioeconomically considered working-class families, in many ways the North End informants cannot be considered completely homogeneous. Apart from the self-evident heterogeneity built into the sample by the inclusion of both males and females, there are social divergencies such as grade-age and ethnicity. All sixty informants were equally divided into first grade (six-year-old) students; fourth grade (ten-year-old) students; and eighth grade (fourteen-year-old) students. Furthermore, all the informants were either monolingual or bilingual speaking children.

The purpose of correlating the linguistic features of the interdental fricatives with various social variables is to demonstrate that these linguistic features are sensitive to social factors or extralinguistic attributes. Although all social variables of grade-age, sex, and ethnicity, and the various combinations of these three variables were exhaustively investigated, only those patterns which proved highly significant are reported here. Therefore, presented in the following sections are the basic social variables of grade-age, sex, and ethnicity, all of which have indicated a high degree of systematic patterning, in addition to two corollary patterns of the combined social variables of sex and ethnicity, and age and ethnicity. The tabulations of the remaining possible combined social variables, namely, age and sex, and age, sex, and ethnicity, failed to demonstrate any consistently patterned sociolinguistic significance. Consequently, these latter two combined social variables have been disregarded throughout the remaining four sections of this chapter.

Covariation with grade-age, sex, and ethnicity. When the grade-age stratification for interdental fricatives was tabulated, it was found that the fourth grade children had the highest frequencies of stigmatized despirantizations, eighth

3   Variable analysis of third person singular present tense verb concord / 55

graders the lowest, and the first graders had intermediate frequencies. The first graders had a despirantization frequency rate of 84.2 percent; fourth graders had the lowest rate of all, 74.8 percent. It may be noted that this patterned distribution by grade-age for interdental fricatives culled from the spontaneous, informal recorded speech samples also proved to be the identical hierarchically ordered pattern in the more formal style of the narrative reading test, the perception-discrimination test, and the word-pair reading test of interdental fricatives.

The tabulation of the social variable of sex for interdental fricatives indicated that males consistently had a higher frequency rate of stigmatized despirantizations (87.3 percent) than females (79.1 percent). One of Wolfram's sociolinguistic conclusions (1969:215) was that female speakers have lower frequencies of the use of stigmatized forms than do male speakers. The North End data verifies Wolfram's findings in his Detroit study.

In correlating ethnicity with despirantization in informal speech, monolingual speakers had higher frequencies of the stigmatized forms. Monolingual children despirantized 88.8 percent whereas bilingual children despirantized 78.2 percent of the time. Table 3.14 indicates the number of despirantizations and their corresponding percentages according to the social variables of grade-age, sex, and ethnicity.

Table 3.14.   Covariation of despirantized interdental fricatives in casual speech with grade-age, sex, and ethnicity

Grade-Age	No. despirantized/ No. observed	Percent despirantized
1	425/505	84.2
4	728/784	92.9
8	581/777	74.8
Total =	1,734/2,066	
Sex		
Males	1,060/1,214	87.3
Females	674/852	79.1
Total =	1,734/2,066	
Ethnicity		
Monolinguals	986/1,110	88.8
Bilinguals	748/956	78.2
Total =	1,734/2,066	

Covariation with sex and ethnicity. The tabulated data for the combined social factor of sex and ethnicity showed that bilingual females had the lowest despirantization frequencies (78.2 percent) of all four groups. Monolingual males had the highest frequencies, 93.9 percent, monolingual females had the second highest, 84.5 percent, and bilingual males had the next highest, 82.5 percent.

Covariation with grade-age and ethnicity. The combined social variables of grade-age and ethnicity also showed a consistent pattern, as may be expected from the highly patterned individual social variables of grade-age and of ethnicity. The despirantized frequency percentages between monolingual and bilingual speakers were generally widespread among first and eighth graders. However, among the monolingual and bilingual speakers in the fourth grade, there was not a noticeable difference.

Narrative Reading Test

The fourth part of the interview with each of the sixty Italian-American informants consisted of the child reading a short narrative reading passage. The selected passage was chosen according to the child's appropriate grade level (see appendix A). This part of the interview usually lasted two to three minutes, depending both on the length of the reading passage and the speed of the reader. The reading passages, which were administered to the North End children in each of the three grades before it was decided just which features would be carefully analyzed, contained varying frequencies of positional occurrences of both voiced and voiceless interdental fricatives. The goal of each of the graded readings was to test the ability of the North End children to read aloud words exhibiting the interdental fricatives, not in isolation as in the word-pairs reading test, but in a contextual narrative form where voiced and voiceless *th* words were couched among a large variety of other words.

Word-initial voiced *th-* was the only commonly shared positional occurrence of *th* in the first, fourth, and eighth grade readings. There were twenty-nine examples of word-initial voiced *th-* in the first grade reading passage; sixteen in the fourth grade reading passage; and thirty-nine in the eighth grade passage. Examples of word-medial voiced *-th-* were present in the fourth grade reading selection (two examples) and in the eighth grade passage (three examples). However, there was only one example of word-initial voiceless *th-* and it was found in the fourth grade passage.[2] Finally, there were five examples of word-final voiceless *-th* in the first grade reading selection and only one example of voiceless *-th* in the eighth grade reading selection.

Covariation with grade-age, sex, and ethnicity. When the total number of ninety-nine voiced and voiceless interdental fricatives, which appeared in varying frequencies in each of the graded readings, were correlated with the social variables, there emerged several significant sociolinguistic patterns. For example, when the grade-age level of the informants was correlated with the number of despirantized interdental fricatives, the results confirmed previous observations in this chapter that the fourth graders had the highest frequency rate of despirantizations, 80.3 percent; the eighth graders the lowest, 72.8 percent; and the first graders had an intermediate frequency of 75.3 percent. Furthermore, when

3 Variable analysis of third person singular present tense verb concord / 57

sexual identity was correlated with the frequency rate of despirantizations, it was found that the difference between males and females was again significant. Males indicated a stronger tendency to despirantize (82.4 percent) than females (67.9 percent). The analysis of the narrative reading selections also indicated that ethnicity seemed to play an important role in despirantization. The ethnicity variable showed that monolingual children had a despirantization frequency rate of 80.5 percent whereas bilingual children had 69.8 percent. Table 3.15 indicates the number of despirantized interdental fricatives according to the grade-age, sex, and ethnicity of all sixty informants. It should be noted that there were thirty-four potential examples of interdental fricatives in the first grade reading passage, thus making 680 the total number of possible realizations for the twenty children in the first grade. There were nineteen potential //ð// and //θ// in the fourth grade selection, thus making 380 possible realizations. The eighth graders read forty-three potential examples of the fricatives, making 860 possible realizations. The total number of all potential realizations is 1,920.

Table 3.15. Covariation of despirantized interdental fricatives in the narrative reading test with grade-age, sex, and ethnicity

Grade-Age	No. despirantized/ No. observed	Percent despirantized
1	512/680	75.3
4	305/380	80.3
8	626/860	72.8
Total =	1,443/1,920	
Sex		
Males	791/960	82.4
Females	652/960	67.9
Total =	1,443/1,920	
Ethnicity		
Monolinguals	773/960	80.5
Bilinguals	670/960	69.8
Total =	1,443/1,920	

Covariation with sex and ethnicity. Of the two corollary patterns which emerged from the covariation analysis, the first pattern confirmed what the previous sociolinguistic correlation also found, namely, that bilingual females had a lower frequency rate of despirantized forms (55.2 percent) than either bilingual males (84.3 percent), monolingual males (80.4 percent), or monolingual females (80.6 percent).

Covariation with grade-age and ethnicity. The other significant corollary pattern was that of grade-age and ethnicity combined variables which showed that the fourth grade monolingual and bilingual children had for all practical purposes identical frequencies of stigmatized forms when they read the reading selection: monolinguals, 81.1 percent; bilinguals, 79.5 percent. The difference in frequency rates for the first grade monolingual (73.5 percent) and bilingual (77.1 percent) readers was only slightly lower than the fourth graders' rates. However, there was a significant difference between monolinguals (88.1 percent) and bilinguals (57.4 percent) in the eighth grade readers' performance.

Word-pair Reading Test

In the sixth part of the interview, each informant was asked to read the same list of forty pairs of words as in the perception test of potential interdental fricatives and their nonstandard variants. It was hoped that the intervening parts of the interview were sufficiently varied to distract the informant from remembering what he or she had heard on the tape recorded reading of the forty pairs. The same list of words was used for the pronunciation-reading exercise for comparative measurement purposes. The goal of this task to read the list of words exhibiting $//ð//-//d//$ and $//θ//-//t//$ was designed to test the correlation between (1) the North End children's ability to audibly perceive and differentiate the above phonological differences and (2) their ability actually to pronounce words exhibiting those specific phonetic features. It should be noted here that only the fourth and eighth grade children participated in this reading exercise. The first grade children did not do so because they had confirmed in the pilot study the expectation that they would find the reading of this list of words a tedious, if not an impossible task.

Since some *th* words were omitted from the perception-discrimination test because they did not manifest the minimal differences between $//ð//-//d//$ or $//θ//-//t//$ (e.g., #12 south-mouth; #15 width-with) as the other twenty-one minimal pairs, each word had to be reclassified according to the familiar positional occurrences of voiced and voiceless *th*. As a result, there were six potential words exhibiting word-initial voiced *th-* (see appendix A: # #8, 9, 14, 17a, 19a, 19b); one potential word-medial voiced *-th-* (#10); four potential word-initial voiceless *th-* (# #17b, 26, 28, 39); two potential word-medial voiceless *-th-* (# #7, 25); and finally, twenty-one potential word-final voiceless *-th* (# #4, 5a, 5b, 12a, 12b, 13, 15a, 15b, 16, 18, 20, 21, 22, 29, 31, 32a, 32b, 33, 37, 38, 40). The thirty-four potential *th* words for each of the forty informants totalled 1,360 possible pronunciations.

The figures in the following pages represent the number of nonstandard despirantized variants of the standard interdental fricatives $//ð//$ and $//θ//$ for both the fourth and eighth graders; that is, the statistics refer to the number of times potential standard $//ð//$ was actually pronounced as nonstandard $//d//$, and potential standard $//θ//$ was actually pronounced as nonstandard $//t//$.

3 Variable analysis of third person singular present tense verb concord / 59

Covariation with grade-age, sex, and ethnicity. The analysis of both the fourth and eighth graders' reading performance of the thirty-four *th* word-pairs indicated that although the fourth graders once again had the highest frequencies of stigmatized despirantizations, the difference percentage-wise according to the grade-age factor was not as significant as the previous two sets of correlations. Fourth graders despirantized *th* words 75.7 percent whereas the eighth graders did so 73.1 percent. However, the sexual identity variable continued to indicate a significant pattern between males and females. Males read *th* words with more stigmatized pronunciations (82.6 percent) than females (66.2 percent). Furthermore, for ethnicity, monolingual speakers tended to read *th* words with slightly more despirantizations (77.1 percent) than did bilinguals (71.8 percent), as Table 3.16 shows.

Table 3.16.   Covariation of despirantized interdental fricatives in the word-pair reading test with grade-age, sex, and ethnicity

Grade-Age	No. despirantized/ No. observed	Percent despirantized
1	X	X
4	515/680	75.7
8	497/680	73.1
Total =	1,012/1,360	
Sex		
Males	562/680	82.6
Females	450/680	66.2
Total =	1,012/1,360	
Ethnicity		
Monolinguals	524/680	77.1
Bilinguals	488/680	71.8
Total =	1,012/1,360	

Covariation with sex and ethnicity. When the combined social variables of sex and ethnicity were compared for the reading test of *th* word-pairs, it was discovered that although the bilingual females had the lowest frequencies (61.8 percent), the monolingual females had the next lowest frequencies (70.6 percent) rather than bilingual males (81.8 percent), as had been the case in the previously observed covariations. Monolingual males continued to have the highest frequencies (83.5 percent).

Covariation with grade-age and ethnicity. In comparing grade-age and ethnicity, similar frequencies of despirantized word-pairs were found among the fourth grade monolinguals, 75.3 percent, and bilingual readers, 76.2 percent. However, eighth grade monolinguals (78.8 percent) and bilinguals (67.4 percent) continued to indicate a definite hierarchically ordered pattern.

Stylistic Variations

Up until the early 1960s, the majority of linguists throughout the world shied away from the problems of stylistic variation, not because these problems were considered irrelevant or so problematic as to rule out any linguistic significance, but rather because they were thought of as unsuitable or inadequate according to the structural school's linguistic criteria and principles for fieldwork methodology advocated by many structuralists prior to the 1960s. In general, structuralists would abstract those unvarying functional units of language whose occurrence can be predicted by linguistic rules. The influence of stylistic conditioning on linguistic behavior was considered to be merely statistical. Consequently, statements of probability rather than detailed and specific rules were judged unscientific by many linguists.

Labov was one of the first linguists to tackle head-on the challenging and elusive problem of stylistic variation. One of Labov's (1966) many insights in his pioneering study of English spoken in New York City was that variations in a number of styles were, indeed, systematized; styles are not merely in an uninhibited state of perpetual flux. Labov not only developed techniques for isolating various styles, but he also correlated linguistic features with each style. His initial exploration of the use of English in New York City pointed the way for other linguists to continue fathoming the sociolinguistic importance and relevance of patterned variation in different styles and contexts of linguistic features. Working with his New York City data, Labov discovered an interesting phenomenon which indicated that in each of the styles, ranging from the least formal to the most formal, there was a gradual decrease in the frequency of socially stigmatized forms as informants would shift from a less formal to a more formal style of speech.

In working with the various kinds of data in the North End project, it was relatively easy to study the range of styles used by each of the three grade-age groups. The first style noted was one marked by a casual, informal, or relaxed manner in which the North End informants spoke about their favorite sports, hobbies, television programs, and so on. This first style of speech used by the informants in the narrative part of the interview is referred to as *casual style*. In this style of speech, in which no attention is directed specifically to the language used, there is less pressure to conform to the Standard American English norm. Another style noted was that of *narrative reading*. All sixty informants read a passage appropriate for each of the three grade levels. In each passage there were a number of occurrences of interdental fricatives. It was found that in the narrative reading style, the North End informants tended to despirantize interdental fricatives less often than in casual style. The third style is characterized by a more deliberate, formal, or careful style of reading a list of minimal word-pairs exemplifying //d̯//-//d// and //θ//-//t// contrasts. In this latter style, called *careful reading style*, there occurred the least number of socially stigmatized despirantizations, presumably because the informant's attention was focused on the reading list as a language performance exercise.

Table 3.17 indicates the percentages of despirantization for each of the three grades according to the three styles: casual, narrative reading, and careful reading. Since the first graders were not capable of reading the voiced and voiceless interdental fricative minimal pairs, no percentage appears in this cell marked for first grade and careful style.

Table 3.17. Covariation of despirantized interdental fricatives in casual, narrative reading, and careful reading styles with grade-age, sex, and ethnicity

Grade	Casual	Narrative reading	Careful reading
1	84.2	75.3	X
4	92.9	80.3	75.7
8	74.8	72.8	73.1
Sex			
Males	87.3	82.4	82.6
Females	79.1	67.9	66.2
Ethnicity			
Monolinguals	88.8	80.5	77.1
Bilinguals	78.2	69.8	71.8

As far as the data in Table 3.17 indicate, fourth graders manifest a wider range of style shifting than either the first or eighth graders. The fourth graders also showed a shift of despirantization as the style changed. In general, linguistic variables show a marked shift from the least formal to the most formal style. As expected, the fourth graders' percentages in Table 3.17 indicate a higher frequency rate of the socially marked stigmatized despirantization in casual speech because, presumably, their attention was not drawn to focus consciously on their language performance. Note that in the more formal style of narrative reading and in the most formal style of the careful reading of isolated minimal word-pairs, the percentage of despirantization drops from 92.9 percent to 80.3 percent, and from 80.3 percent to 75.7 percent. The first graders despirantized more interdental fricatives in casual style than in the narrative reading style.

The absence of any strong tendency among the eighth graders to decrease despirantization as they progressed to more formal styles of narrative reading and careful reading is, to say the least, quite puzzling. It is definitely an anomaly that the data for each of the three styles used by the eighth graders reflect a despirantization frequency mean of 73.6 percent (74.8, 72.8, 73.1 percents). After carefully analyzing the data, no apparent motivation for such an unexpected departure from the stylistic pattern emerged. There are no clear answers explaining this linguistic behavior of the eighth graders. One possible explanation, however, may be that eighth graders tend to be less inhibited than either first or fourth graders by social pressures to conform to "acceptable" standards of speech.

Figure 2 displays the frequency rates in percentages for despirantization for three styles for each of the grades.

Figure 2. Despirantization in three styles according to grade-age

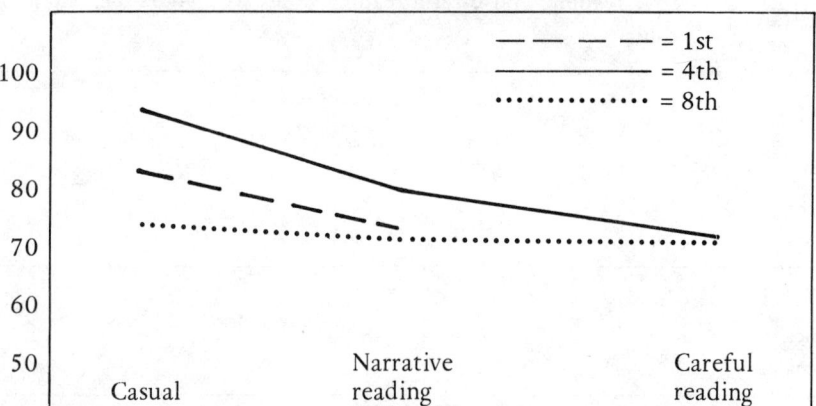

When sex was studied in relationship to the three styles, the data for the frequencies of despirantization indicated in Table 3.17 show that fewer despirantizations occurred in the narrative reading style than in casual style for both males and females. However, when there was a shift from narrative reading style to careful reading style of minimal word-pairs, there was no well-defined, stratified decrease in the frequency of despirantization; in fact, in one instance (71.8 percent), there was a slight increase of despirantization. The same phenomenon occurred when ethnicity was investigated, as Table 3.17 shows.

An hypothesis for the undifferentiated frequency rates between narrative reading and careful reading styles is that the informant considers any kind of reading exercise as a formal task in which he is on exhibition. The North End child may generally look upon his reading performance as a speech setting in which his speech is being monitored by a critical listener, whether the listener is a teacher, a fellow student, or a sociolinguistic researcher. Thus, it seems reasonable to suggest that both the reading of the narrative passage from a graded reader and from a list of minimal word-pairs may be looked upon by North End children as an equally (i.e. undifferentiated) formalized speech setting. Therefore, there is a possibility that there may not be any significant stylistic variation at all between narrative reading and careful reading styles.

3 Variable analysis of third person singular present tense verb concord / 63

Perception-Discrimination Test

In the third part of the interview with all sixty Italian-American informants, each child was asked to listen carefully to a prepared tape which contained an assorted list of randomly selected pairs of words. The majority of these words were composed of voiced and voiceless interdental fricatives in initial, medial, and final positions (see appendix A). A detailed description of this perception-discrimination test is given in Chapter 1. However, to summarize briefly, the goals of this test were for each informant to listen, discriminate, and then judge whether or not any given pair of words sounded the same or sounded different. The speaker who tape recorded the forty assorted pairs of words was a Standard American English speaker born, raised, and educated in Chicago, Illinois. All sixty Italian-American children were asked to listen carefully for any significant difference between each pair of words; to judge whether or not there was indeed any difference between the two words; and then to circle the appropriate letter: S, if a pair of words sounded the *same*; or D, if a pair of words sounded *different*.

It was hypothesized that since the majority of the North End children had a very strong tendency to despirantize //d̶// and //θ// when they spoke informally and casually, they were more likely than not unaware of the difference between //d̶//-//d// and //θ//-//t// and could not, therefore, audibly perceive the sound difference between the interdental fricatives and the apico-alveolar stops. For example, in number four of the perception-discrimination test, the minimal pair, *boat-both*, occurs. In Standard American English, the final consonant in *boat* is pronounced as a voiceless apico-alveolar stop and the final consonant in *both* as a voiceless interdental fricative. A speaker of Standard American English not only hears the difference between *boat* and *both* and attributes different meanings to each word, but he also pronounces these words differently: [bout] for *boat* and [bouθ] for *both*. However, the North End children pronounce *both* and *boat* with the identical pronunciations: [bout]. It was hypothesized that nonstandard speaking Italian-American children of the North End do not always perceive the difference between //d̶//-//d// and //θ//-//t// when hearing these sounds. This hypothesis was proven true based on the statistical results of all analyzed pairs of words in the perception-discrimination test.

The first three pairs of words in the test (*sky-fly, dog-frog, days-daze*) were selected in order to determine whether or not the child had understood the instructions given him or her on the tape recording. Each child was closely observed when he or she responded to the first three pairs of words. It is interesting to note that no child found any difficulty in understanding the task of the perception-discrimination test primarily because all the children had already been exposed to this type of 'Same' or 'Different' technique in their ordinary school work and were consequently familiar with the test's operational procedures. The answers to these 'dummy' pairs of words, which were successful in determining the procedural instructions, were not included in any of the tabulated data.

Included within the list of forty pairs of words were nine sets of words which were randomly distributed to distract the informant from inferring that the point of this test was to differentiate //đ//-//d// and //θ//-//t// in minimal pairs. The nine pairs of words used to distract the informants were: (6) *glue-glow*; (11) *wheat-wet*; (23) *bite-bait*; (24) *float-flop*; (27) *book-bike*; (30) *willow-pillow*; (34) *flop-flock*; (35) *ask-ax*; (36) *show-flow*. In addition, there were two pairs of words which were repeated twice in order to test the consistency of the informants' responses, namely, (4) and (33) *boat-both*; and (22) and (40) *pat-path*.[3]

The following twenty-one randomly selected pairs of potentially perceivable words having //đ// or //θ// were divided into initial, medial, and final positions.

Word-initial voiced *th*-:

(8) then-den
(9) dose-those
(14) this-dis

Word-medial voiced -*th*-:

(10) mother-mudder

Word-initial voiceless *th*-:

(26) thank-tank
(28) tin-thin
(39) three-tree

Word-medial voiceless -*th*-:

(7) batroom-bathroom
(25) faithful-fateful

Word-final voiceless -*th*:

(4) boat-both   (22) pat-path
(13) math-mat   (29) wit-with
(16) faith-fate   (31) myth-mitt
(18) boot-booth   (33) boat-both
(20) rat-wrath   (37) North-nort
(21) toot-tooth   (40) pat-path

The two pairs of words found in (3) *days-daze* and (5) *path-path* sound the *same* in Standard American English and all other word-pairs sound *different* in Standard American English.[4]

In the following pages, discussion is focused on the analysis of the above potentially perceivable twenty-one minimal pairs. The statistics given in the following tables reflect two facts. First, they reflect to what degree the North End children are capable of perceiving, discriminating, and judging the minimal pairs of words with //đ//-//d// and //θ//-//t// as sounding different when in fact they sound different in Standard American English. In other words, the statistics

3 Variable analysis of third person singular present tense verb concord / 65

indicate the number and percent of perceived and discriminated differentiated sound contrasts between //d̲//-//d// and //θ//-//t// in relationship to nonlinguistic, social variables such as (1) grade-age, (2) sex, and (3) ethnicity, and the combined social variables of (4) sex and ethnicity, and finally, (5) grade-age and ethnicity. The overall frequency rate of perceptibility for all sixty North End informants, regardless of their specific social factors such as grade-age, sex, and ethnicity, was 56.4 percent (or 711/1,260).

Covariation with grade-age, sex, and ethnicity. When grade-age stratification for the perception-discrimination test of interdental fricatives was tabulated, it was found that fourth graders had the lowest frequencies of perceptibility (46.4 percent), the eighth graders the highest (63.8 percent), and first graders had an intermediate percentage of perceptibility (59.0 percent).

The North End males found greater difficulty (49.4 percent) in perceiving the differences between //d̲//-//d// and //θ//-//t// than did the females (63.5 percent). The correlation of sexual identity to the frequency of perceptibility indicated that the males had a stronger tendency not to discriminate the sound difference between the interdental fricatives and the apico-alveolar stops.

There was also a great disparity between monolingual and bilingual Italian-American children for the ethnicity variable. Monolingual children had a perceptibility frequency rate of 46.8 percent whereas bilingual children had 66.0 percent. The figures for all three basic social variables are shown in Table 3.18.

Table 3.18. Covariation of despirantized interdental fricatives in the perception-discrimination test with grade-age, sex, and ethnicity

Grade-Age	No. discriminated/ No. examples	Percent discriminated
1	248/420	59.0
4	195/420	46.4
8	268/420	63.8
Total =	711/1,260	
Sex		
Males	311/630	49.4
Females	400/630	63.5
Total =	711/1,260	
Ethnicity		
Monolinguals	295/630	46.8
Bilinguals	416/630	66.0
Total =	711/1,260	

Covariation with sex and ethnicity. The comparison of the combined nonlinguistic variables of sexual identity and ethnicity with the frequencies of perceptibility also proved to have systematic patterning. Once again, bilingual females had the highest frequencies, 71.7 percent, with monolingual males (38.4 percent), monolingual females (55.2 percent), and bilingual males (60.3 percent) following previously observed hierarchical patterns.

Covariation with grade-age and ethnicity. Grade-age and ethnicity correlation were again found to be patterned according to previous observations. There were only slight percentage differences between fourth grade monolinguals (42.9 percent) and bilinguals (50.0 percent), whereas there were three striking differences between first grade monolinguals (51.0 percent) and bilinguals (67.1 percent), and eighth grade monolinguals (46.7 percent) and bilinguals (81.0 percent).

Comparative measurements. Several observations can be made regarding the systematic patterns found in the contrastive analysis of both the perception-discrimination and the word-pair reading test results. First, although the first grade children were not capable of reading the word-pairs and were consequently excluded from this part of the interview, both sets of tests nevertheless indicated that the fourth graders had a much stronger tendency than the eighth graders not to distinguish audibly between //ð//-//d// and //θ//-//t// as well as not to pronounce these phonetic differences. Second, sexual identity showed a consistent pattern in that males in both tests had higher frequencies of despirantization imperceptibility and pronunciations than females. Third, for ethnicity, monolinguals indicated a stronger tendency not to discriminate audibly the phonetic differences between interdental fricatives and apico-alveolar stops and not to pronounce them correctly. Fourth, when the sexual identity and ethnicity factors were compared, bilingual females were noted to have the greatest ability to perceive and differentiate the fricatives from the stops, as well as to produce them with their standardized realizations.

Summary

After careful investigation of the phenomenon of interdental fricative despirantization among the North End children, it is clear that despirantization occurs variably among both male and female monolingual and bilingual speakers ranging in age from six to ten to fourteen years who are in the first, fourth, and eighth grades, respectively. The North End data revealed not only that frequency rates for the widely recognized socially stigmatized linguistic feature *th* were very high in each of its positional occurrences, but they also yielded variable rules for each of the positional occurrences of *th*. Furthermore, four different sets of sociolinguistic correlations pointed out consistently the fact that more males despirantized //ð// and //θ// than females; a tendency which substantiated a number of previous studies regarding sexual identity related to nonstandard usage. The results of the linguistic analysis of the informal or spontaneous conversations with the informants and the three administered tests also indicated that monolinguals have a relatively greater tendency to despirantize interdental fricatives than bilinguals. Furthermore, perhaps contrary to general expectations was the phenomenon that fourth graders were consistently characterized by higher frequencies of the socially stigmatized variants //d// and //t// than the first graders. It would normally be expected that because the first graders had learned their dialects more recently within their environments and because they did not have the exposure to as many varied dialects spoken by older children, adolescents, and adults both within and without the North End as the older ten-year-old (fourth grade) and fourteen-year-old (eighth grade) informants, they would consequently have much higher frequency levels of nonstandard realizations than the fourth and eighth graders. This and other similar problems dealing with the correlations between linguistic and extralinguistic variables will be discusses in much greater detail in Chapter 8.

When stylistic variations were analyzed in relationship to both despirantization and the social variables, it was found that there was generally a marked decrease in despirantization as there was a corresponding shift from casual style to narrative reading style. However, there was no consistently marked decrease of despirantization when there was a shift from narrative reading style to careful reading style, which leads to a considered possibility that North End children look upon any form of reading exercise as indicative of an undifferentiated, equally formalized speech setting and style.

4
Variable Analysis of Word-Final Consonant Cluster Simplification

General Remarks

In casual or spontaneous speech behavior, most speakers of American English tend to simplify words ending with a consonant cluster by deleting the final member of the consonant cluster. Nonstandard speakers, such as the North End Italian-American children, have a greater tendency to reduce or simplify word-final consonant clusters than do standard speakers. For example, the Italian-American children speaking nonstandard English say words such as *feast, mask, priest, soft,* and *band* by pronouncing them as *feas, mass, pries, sof,* and *ban* respectively. Because of this phenomenon, we found that pairs of words such as *Mass* and *mask, class* and *clasp, soul* and *sold* have identical pronunciations in the dialects in the majority of the North End children.

Whether a person is speaking Standard English or nonstandard variants of English, consonant cluster simplification is encouraged when certain phonological environments are present. For example, when a consonant cluster is followed by a word beginning with a consonant, the following consonant becomes so conducive to cluster simplification in many American English dialects that the final member of the preceding consonant cluster is frequently reduced to a single consonant as in the sentence:

> Like on the las(t) *n*ight of the big feas(t) *w*hen the pries(t) *c*omes to bless the ol(d) statue of St. Anthony, all the people sing those religious songs. (23)

There are other environments such as a following vowel or a following utterance pause which do not favor the simplification of the preceding consonant cluster; in fact, if simplification occurs in these environments, it becomes a well-defined indicator of socially stigmatized speech. In Table 4.1, examples are given for consonant cluster simplification for Standard American English and for the nonstandard North End variant of American English when a consonant, vowel, and pause follow a consonant cluster.

Table 4.1. Comparison of the potential effect on simplification of a following consonant, vowel, and pause in both Standard and nonstandard American English

	___##C	___##V	___##
Standard American English	bes' man	best idea	best.
Nonstandard Italian-American English	bes' man	bes' idea	bes.

In-depth research on word-final consonant cluster simplification of various nonstandard varieties of American English has been carried out. For example, Black English has been extensively studied by Labov et al. (1968), Wolfram (1969), and Fasold (1972). It was found in each of their respective studies that only when certain phonological environments are present will there be a quantitatively higher tendency for noncategorical, systematic variation in the reduction or simplification of word-final consonant clusters. Furthermore, these linguists, working independently with data from three widely separated cities, New York, Detroit, and Washington, D.C., have come to many of the same conclusions about the specific phonological constraints for cluster simplification for both standard and nonstandard speakers of English.

Procedures

Before examining the consonant cluster data of the North End Italian-American monolingual and bilingual children, it is first necessary to describe the procedures used in extracting and tabulating these data. The methodology of gathering the data has already been described in detail in Chapter 1; but briefly, twenty examples of potential word-final consonant clusters were extracted for each speaker and each example was transcribed phonetically. The consonant cluster data under consideration included nouns, verbs, adjectives, and adverbs.

It is essential to note here the important distinction which was originally made by Wolfram and Fasold (1970:43-44) regarding two basic types of clusters which are affected by the phonological processes of word-final consonant cluster simplification. First, consonant clusters are reduced only when both members of the cluster belong to the same base word as in *first, mask, clasp,* and *cold*. Second, there are clusters which can be simplified when the past tense suffix, *-ed*, is added to the base word only if certain phonological constraints are present. In all varieties of American English, the *-ed* suffix has three phonetic forms, [ɨd], [t], and [d], and each of these three forms depends on how the base word ends. If the base word should end in *t* or *d*, then the *-ed* suffix is pronounced [ɨd] so that *mounted* and *befriended* are actually pronounced as [mauntɨd] and [bifrɛndɨd], respectively. If the base word ends in a voiceless consonant, then the cluster ends in [t] so that *chopped* and *yanked* are actually pronounced as [cʰapt] and [yaɛŋkt], respectively. Finally, if the base word ends in a voiced sound, it is pronounced [d] so that words like *killed* and *canned* are actually pronounced as [kʰIld] and [kʰɛnd], respectively. Therefore, when the past tense *-ed* suffix marker occurs in either a voiced or voiceless cluster, then this cluster may be simplified by removing the final member of the cluster segment only when certain phonological constraints are present. Moreover, it should be noted that the North End data include only those verb bases which end in consonantal segments except [t] and [d]. Since verb bases ending in [t] and [d] take the suffix form [ɨd], no consonant cluster ever occurs. Also to be noted is that thirty-six examples were eliminated from the final number of 822 examples of consonant clusters because it could not be determined whether the final stop was present or not. In the majority of the cases where a phonetic [t] or [d] was present, it was uncertain if the [t] or [d] segment represented the past tense suffix marker *-ed* or the initial [t] or [d] of the following word. The two following examples illustrate the problem.

(1) My brother was *asked to* go to the party, but he didn't go; he *slammed the* door when he left the house. (47)
(2) My teacher made us stay after school and she *talked to* us for fifteen minutes. (17)

There remained 122 clear cases of verb bases ending in nonapico alveolar consonants in which the *-ed* suffix was expected.

A list of examples representing the two types of consonant clusters which are capable of being simplified is given in Table 4.2. This list, comparable to the one complied by Wolfram and Fasold (1970:45) in their study of Black English, represents actual consonant cluster combinations found in the North End data. There are two types of consonant clusters: Type I represents those clusters which do not involve the past tense suffix marker, *-ed*, and Type II represents clusters which result from the addition of the *-ed* suffix.

It is important to note that certain consonant clusters have not been included in this list in Table 4.2, such as [mp] (e.g. *jump, swamp, pump*); [nt] (e.g. *Saint, front, aunt*); [lt] (e.g. *Walt, fault, built*); [rt] (e.g. *hurt, Bert, flirt*); [nk] (e.g. *pink, rink, mink*); [ŋk] (e.g. *bank, flank, rank*); and [lp] (e.g. *help. gulp, pulp*). The reason is basically a phonological one. According to Wolfram's and Fasold's studies on standard and several nonstandard variants of American English, the consonant cluster simplification rule operates when, and only when, both members of the cluster are either voiced or unvoiced. Words like *find, mind, old*, and *mold* end in two voiced sounds, [n] and [d], or [l] and [d]. However, words like *felt, rump*, and *fink* end in one voiced and one voiceless sound. The sounds [l], [m], and [n] are voiced whereas [t], [p], and [k] are voiceless. Therefore, word-final consonant clusters are reduced only when two conditions are met: (1) the second member of the cluster must be a nonstrident stop (e.g. not an affricate) and (2) the two members must agree in voicing.

Table 4.2. Consonant clusters in which the final member of the cluster may be absent

Phonetic cluster*	Type I	Type II
[st]	feast, lost, fist	chased, dressed, kissed
[sp]	rasp, wasp, clasp	
[sk]	wisk, flask, risk	
[št]		mashed, finished, crashed
[zd]		supposed, raised, composed
[ǰd]		judged, barged, charged
[ft]	left, loft, gift	cuffed, roughed, laughed
[vd]		believed, loved, moved
[nd]	kind, mind, found	opened, warned, turned
[ld]	old, cold, mild	peeled, pulled, whistled
[pt]	kept, except, overslept	taped, popped, jumped
[kt]	act, inspect, except	frisked, masked, picked

*Where there are no examples under Type I or II, the cluster does not occur under that category.

In summary, in word-final position, consonant clusters which share the same voicing specifications are sometimes reduced in Standard English and frequently reduced in nonstandard varieties of English. This pattern of consonant cluster simplification affects a number of different clusters including sonorant + stop, stop + stop, and spirant + stop clusters.

The number of clear examples of consonant clusters found in the Italian-American speech of the North End children was tabulated as 822. Of this total, 329 clusters (or 40.0 percent) were simplified whereas the remaining 493 clusters (or 60.0 percent) were left intact.

Constraints on Consonant Cluster Simplification

The data from the spontaneous conversations taken from the interviews with the Italian-American children indicate that the major constraint affecting cluster simplification had to do with the environment following the potential simplified cluster. It is a well-established fact that among many variants of American English, what follows the consonant cluster is the essential linguistic environment which favors or inhibits cluster simplification. It is clear from Table 4.3 that if the word following a cluster begins with a vowel, fewer clusters will become simplified than if there is no following word as in the case of terminal junction or utterance pause. It is also clear from Table 4.3 that the condition favoring consonant cluster simplification is the environment in which a consonant follows the cluster.

Table 4.3. Comparison of the effect of three following environments of both monomorphemic and bimorphemic cluster simplification in the speech of Italian-American children

	___##V	___##	___##C
Intact	214	79	200
Simplified	29	26	274
Percent simplified	11.9	24.8	57.8

N = 822
X^2 = 152.49 $p < .001$

Wolfram (1969:61) claims in his study of Detroit Black English that a following pause affects consonant cluster simplification in the same way as does a following vowel. However, Labov et al. (1968:136) and Fasold (1972:66-67), working with their respective sets of Black English data, reached the opposite conclusion. Both Labov's data and Fasold's indicate that pause affects cluster simplification in the same way that a consonant does. Neither Labov nor Wolfram, however, presents evidence to substantiate his conclusions. Fasold, on the other hand, does verify his argument by displaying his empirical data from his Washington, D.C., lower socioeconomic working class Black English informants. In comparing Fasold's Washington data to the North End data, some striking contrasts can be quickly seen. The Washington data of 382 examples of bimorphemic clusters indicate that the effect of a pause and consonant are, for all practical purposes, almost statistically identical. When consonant clusters are followed by a pause, they become simplified 73.0 percent of the time; when consonant clusters are followed by a consonant, they become simplified 76.2 percent of the time. However, the North End data of 303 bimorphemic clusters indicate clear-cut gradations among all three following phonological environments of vowel, pause, and consonant. As indicated in Table 4.4, more clusters tend to become simplified when they are followed by a consonant (39.1 percent) than when followed by a pause (25.7 percent). A following vowel greatly reduces the effect of simplifying or reducing the preceding consonant cluster (13.4 percent).

Table 4.4 shows that both the Washington, D.C., and the North End data agree substantially that a following consonant tends to favor cluster simplification and a following vowel tends to inhibit cluster simplification. However, unlike Fasold's data, the North End data make it quite clear that pause functions differently from consonants in affecting clusters. The North End data cannot justify the dichotomy suggested by Labov and his associates (1968:136) and confirmed by Fasold (1972:67-68) that the following environment of consonant clusters be separated into vowels and nonvowels (or the absence of vowels). The

Table 4.4. Comparison of the effect of three following environments on word-final bimorphemic cluster simplification from Black English speakers from Washington, D.C., and from Italian-American speakers from Boston's North End

	___##V	___##	___##C
Washington, D.C. Black English speakers			
Intact	144	10	34
Simplified	58	27	109
Percent simplified	28.7	73.0	76.2
Boston's North End Italian-American speakers			
Intact	97	26	95
Simplified	15	9	61
Percent simplified	13.4	25.7	39.1

differences in percentages among vowels, pause, and consonants in the Italian-American speakers are too disparate to warrant any further phonological conjoining. Therefore, the results of all analyses of the following environment for all consonant clusters have determined that each of the three types of environments—pause, vowel, and consonant—must be accounted for in the speech of the Italian-American children.

One final observation can be made on the basis of Table 4.4. In his work with second generation Puerto Rican teenagers in New York City's Harlem, Wolfram (1974) studied the cultural and linguistic behavior of several groups with varying social intercourse with black adolescents. One group of Puerto Rican informants with 'restricted black contact' is very similar to the bilingual Italian-American children of the North End in a number of ways which include both their respective cultural and linguistic past backgrounds as well as their present environments. Both groups are second generation children of immigrant parents. Both groups have learned to speak the language of their parents as their first language. Finally, both groups are living in a heavily pronounced ethnic environment with which they identify in a positive way. There are, however, some obvious differences between the two second generation groups. There were only three informants in Wolfram's Puerto Rican group who represented the cultural and linguistic 'restricted contact with blacks.' The North End informants, who also have had limited contacts with blacks, numbered thirty. More significant, however, is the fact that the three Puerto Rican informants were all males of teenage years. The thirty Italian-American bilingual informants were made up of fifteen males and fifteen females whose ages began at approximately six years (ten informants in the first grade), to ten years (ten informants in the fourth grade), and on to fourteen years (ten informants in the eighth grade).

Although both groups share the common Romance language heritage and also share many common cultural traits such as the Roman Catholic religion, a tight-knit nuclear type of family relationship, and a homogeneous immigrant-clustered neighborhood, when both groups were compared as to the influence of the following phonological environments, the North End informants had a significantly lower frequency rate of consonant cluster simplifications than the Puerto Rican informants, as Table 4.5 indicates.

Table 4.5. Comparison of the effect of the following environment of nonconsonants and consonants in New York's Harlem Puerto Rican speakers and Boston's North End Italian-American speakers

	## nonconsonants	## consonants
Bilingual Puerto Ricans		
Intact	64	6
Simplified	48	66
Percent simplified	42.9	91.7
Bilingual Italian-Americans		
Intact	76	48
Simplified	18	102
Percent simplified	19.1	68.0

It was hypothesized that there were at least two probable causes for this difference in the frequencies of cluster simplification among the Puerto Rican teenagers and among the Italian-American grade-school-aged males and females. First, since there was a significant age difference between the Puerto Rican teenagers and the Italian-American first, fourth, and eighth graders, especially the six- and ten-year-old children, it was hypothesized that as each of the teenage Puerto Rican boys had physically and socially matured in his early teenage years, there was a strongly felt need to self-identify with an older but non-adult age group of similar Puerto Rican speakers. As a result of this self-identification with the older, already assimilated group of adolescent speakers, younger teenagers began to alter their linguistic performance to suit the expectations of the older, more established, and governing teenage Puerto Rican boys. On the other hand, the North End children have had considerably less contact with older North End teenagers. Second and more obviously, Wolfram's informants were exclusively males whereas of the thirty North End bilingual informants, fifteen were females. Various studies have already shown that females tend to adopt or integrate nonstandard variant forms at a slower rate than males. Therefore, it was concluded that the lower frequencies of consonant cluster simplifications among the bilingual Italian-American children were due to two possible causes: (1) the relatively isolated social interactions among the Italian-American grade-school-aged males and females, and (2) the tendency of females to integrate nonstandard forms at a relatively slower and less dramatic rate than boys.

A second possible constraint on cluster simplification which was investigated was the effect of monomorphemic and bimorphemic clusters. In their geographically distinct but linguistically related studies, Labov et al. (1968), and Wolfram (1969), and Fasold (1972) discovered that one major constraint on consonant cluster simplification was that bimorphemic clusters (i.e., clusters which have a morpheme boundary between their members) were less often simplified than monomorphemic clusters which do not have any morpheme boundary between their members. For example, the final [t] in *passed* [pas#t# #] is less likely to be absent than the final [t] of *past* [past# #]. Although Wolfram found that the presence of a morpheme boundary was the second most favored constraint, he made no attempt to hierarchize the constraints he found. But Wolfram's analyses of the Detroit data on the cross products percentages indicate that the morpheme boundary was the second most favored constraint while the absence of a following constraint was the alpha or the highest ranked constraint affecting the promotion of cluster simplification. Of the 822 potential consonant clusters tabulated from the spontaneous speech interviews of the North End children, monomorphemic clusters were simplified 48.2 percent (or 250/519) whereas bimorphemic consonant clusters were simplified 26.1 percent (or 79/303). The North End data confirm previous studies made (Wolfram 1969; Fasold 1972) on nonstandard American English that monomorphemic clusters tend to become simplified more frequently than do bimorphemic clusters.

In analyzing the speech of various adolescent groups in New York City, Labov et al. (1968:12) addressed themselves to the problem of final [t] and [d] deletion with verbs such as *tell-told, hold-held, sleep-slept*. This class of verbs signals the past tense by a vowel change and the addition of a final [t] or [d]. Labov's New York City data indicated that the frequency of cluster deletion of these past tense clusters, (e.g. *slept, held, left*), was lower than the frequency of simplification of monomorphemic clusters but higher than the frequency of bimorphemic clusters when a vowel change was not involved.

Working with his Washington data, Fasold found similar results after analyzing verb past tenses. Fasold (1972:72) discovered that of seventy potential clusters having a vowel change and the addition of final [t] or [d], fifty-six (or 80.0 percent) had simplified clusters. Of the 312 examples of verbs which form the past tense only by the suffixation of [t] or [d], 138 (or 44.2 percent) had simplified clusters. The analysis of the North End data revealed that for all practical purposes, the North End children had identical frequency rates of cluster simplification (43.4 percent) when compared to Fasold's Washington speakers (44.2 percent) for regularly formed past tense suffixation. However, for vowel change verbs, there was considerable divergency between the North End speakers (30.4 percent) and Fasold's Washington speakers (80.0 percent). However, the Chi-square test showed that the figures in Table 4.6 were not statistically significant.

Table 4.6. Comparison of the effect of vowel change and the absence of vowel change on word-final bimorphemic cluster simplification among the North End children

	No vowel change	Vowel change
Intact	69	55
Simplified	53	24
Percent simplified	43.4	30.4

N = 201

X^2 = 2.93 (not significant)

The final procedure in analyzing the presence or absence of consonant clusters was to examine all potential bimorphemic clusters in terms of determining to what extent, if any, deletion was favored if the final syllable was unaccented. Fasold (1972:73) found that weak accent favored deletion of [t] and [d] as the second member of bimorphemic clusters (70.0 percent), while for verbs having stressed syllables, deletion was only 41.6 percent. Therefore, Fasold's data indicated that the past tense -ed suffix is significantly more likely to be absent in verbs like *handicapped* and *salvaged* than in verbs like *popped* or *kissed*.

Before the North End data were tabulated for the effect of stressed and nonstressed syllables, it was necessary to remove all examples of verbs which form their past tense by a vowel change as well as the addition of a [t] or [d] since all such verbs are monosyllabic and, therefore, are necessarily accented. This vowel change constraint would obviously affect the tabulation of stressed syllables but not the unstressed syllables. Of the remaining 218 examples, twenty-six had final unaccented syllables, while the remaining 192 ended in or consisted of an accented syllable. Simplified clusters occurred in 57.7 percent of the unstressed syllables but in only 27.6 percent (or 53/192) of the stressed syllables. This difference was significant, but only at the .01 level of confidence, as Table 4.7 shows.

Thus far we have examined all word-final consonant clusters and their following environments. We have examined the effect of the cluster itself in terms of its linguistic complexity, that is, whether the cluster is monomorphemic or

Table 4.7. Comparison of the effect of stress and the absence of stress on final biomorphemic cluster simplification

	Stressed syllables	Unstressed syllables
Intact	139	11
Simplified	53	15
Percent simplified	27.6	57.7
N = 218		
$X^2 = 8.30$ $p < .01$		

bimorphemic. We may now divide the consonant cluster further on the basis of the types of segments involved in the potential cluster simplification process; namely, the phonetic quality of the first member of the cluster. In analyzing the North End data, three major kinds of consonants were investigated for their effect on cluster simplification: sonorant + stop, stop + stop, and spirant + stop. As shown in Table 4.8, final stops were deleted after sonorants 29.1 percent of the time; the frequency of deletion after stops was 19.4 percent and after spirants 50.5 percent. The figures shown in Table 4.8 were highly significant at the .001 level of confidence.

Table 4.8. Comparison of the effect of three types of preceding consonants on word-final monomorphemic and bimorphemic cluster simplification

	Sonorant ##	Stop ##	Spirant ##
Intact	127	116	247
Simplified	52	28	252
Percent simplified	29.1	19.4	50.5
N = 822			
$X^2 = 56.98$ $p < .001$			

It is clear from Table 4.8 that deletion after sonorants is intermediate between deletion after stops and deletion after spirants. Fasold's analysis (1972:71) of the consonant preceding the deletable consonant in the Washington data is similar in some respects to the analysis of the North End data. Fasold's analysis as well as the North End analysis exhibited similar results regarding stop + stop clusters. Fasold's data revealed that Washington, D.C., speakers of Black English deleted stop + stop clusters 37.4 percent of the time while the North End Italian-American speakers deleted stop + stop clusters 19.4 percent of the time. In both sets of data, stop + stop clusters exhibited the lowest percentage of deletion of the final member of consonant clusters. While

Fasold found that sonorant + stop clusters were the most favored environment to become simplified, 63.3 percent, with spirant + stop clusters the second most favorable, 49.1 percent, the Italian-American data revealed that spirant + stop clusters were the most favorable environment to become simplified, 50.5 percent, and sonorant + stop clusters were the next most favored, 29.1 percent. In addition to presenting empirical evidence to ground his findings, Fasold also explains the promotion of cluster simplification after sonorants on general, common phonological reasoning.

> Clearly, 'stopness' and obstruence inhibit deletion, while sustained airstream and sonorance favor it. Stops, which incorporate both the inhibiting factors, cause the lowest level of deletion frequency. Sonorants, which have the two favoring features, cause the greatest frequency. Spirants are obstruent, tending to lower deletion frequency, and sustained, tending to raise it. Not only are these results statistically significant for the Washington data and reasonably convergent with Wolfram's Detroit analysis, but they also make good phonetic sense as well. (Fasold 1972:71).

Labov and his associates in their study of New York City Black English found results comparable to the North End data, namely, that sonorant + stop clusters were not simplified as often as Fasold's spirant + stop deletions. Labov, however, seems to state his findings without offering any verification. 'Finally, we note that clusters with sonorant first members show less simplification than those with obstruent first members' (Labov et al. 1968:135). According to Fasold, there may be a reasonable explanation to Labov's lower deletion rate for sonorant + stop clusters. Labov generalizes his constraints by combining stops and spirants as obstruents and then compares obstruents with sonorants. Furthermore, Labov's sonorant category did not include the consonant [n] because he found [nd] clusters hard to tabulate due to the imperceptibility factor in distinguishing nasality.

> In the case of nasal /n/ plus /-t,d/, we frequently find that a nasal flap is formed in which the stop feature is expressed by the ballistic flap character and the nasal by nasality. Yet this flap characteristic shades imperceptibility into a single nasal, and it was found impossible to code the series satisfactorily: that is, the number of indeterminate cases was large as compared to the clear cases. (Labov et al. 1968:126)

Because Labov combines stops and spirants into one class called 'obstruents' in addition to omitting all [nd] clusters in the tabulations, Fasold argues that Labov's analysis of the preceding obstruents would undoubtedly favor simplification more than would preceding sonorants. Fasold notes further that presumably Labov included [lt] clusters which Wolfram and Fasold deliberately excluded on grounds of their 'mixed voicing' criterion. Since [lt] clusters would be less likely to be reduced than sonorant + [d] clusters, including the [lt] clusters would tend to lower the tabulations of frequency of deletion for sonorant + stop clusters in Labov's data. Another reason why Labov found a lower frequency of deletion after sonorants might be because he included [rd] clusters which tend to lower the deletion frequency for sonorant + stop clusters.

Both [lt] and [rd] clusters have been omitted from the North End data for reasons already mentioned: mixed voicing for [lt] clusters and vowel-like quality of [r] in [rd] clusters. Although [nd] and [ld] were the only kind of sonorant + stop clusters found in the North End data, clusters ending in a sonorant + stop were the second highest in deletion frequency, 29.1 percent, with deletion after spirants as the most favored, 50.5 percent. Of the 179 examples of sonorant + stop clusters analyzed, only two types were found: [nd] as in *bind, blind, friend*, and *stand*, and [ld] as in *told, called, wild*, and *cold*. Fasold (1972:72) discovered that bimorphemic verb [nd] clusters were more often simplified than other sonorant + [d] clusters. The Italian-American data tend to confirm Fasold's analysis because it was found that the North End children deleted more [nd] clusters (35.3 percent) than [ld] clusters (16.0 percent).

Determining the hierarchy of constraints. The procedure in deciding how to hierarchize constraints in variable rule theory, as it has thus far been developed, is to examine all the crucial cross products. In analyzing consonant clusters in terms of establishing a hierarchy of constraints, all three preceding environments, sonorant + stop, stop + stop, and spirant + stop were compared to the following environments of vowel, pause, and consonant. The preceding clusters were also analyzed in their respective monomorphemic and bimorphemic categories. The cross product percentages of preceding and following environments of both monomorphemic and bimorphemic clusters can be seen in Table 4.9.

Like Labov's, Wolfram's, and Fasold's respective analyses of consonant cluster simplification, the analysis of the North End data indicated that a following consonant was the most important single constraint in cluster simplification and that monomorphemic clusters were the next most favored constraint. The remaining potential constraints that were yet to be determined were the preceding consonants, whether sonorants, stops, or spirants. When Table 4.9 is studied carefully, it becomes apparent that no definite, well-ordered hierarchy of constraints is established because of serious deviances which are marked by an asterisk.

Because a well-ordered hierarchy was absent in Table 4.9, further reanalysis of the preceding environment became necessary. It has already been pointed out that only [nd] and [ld] sonorant + stop clusters were found in the speech of the Italian-American children. Attempts were made to find a linguistic common denominator for both the [n] and [l] in order to establish a more generalized category to account for sonorants. According to Chomsky and Halle (1968:302), all sonorants are minus continuant. Since [n] is a sonorant, and hence, -continuant, it was decided to analyze [l] in terms of being -continuant. In Chomsky and Halle's *The Sound Pattern of English* (1968), the authors point

Table 4.9. Cross products of potential constraints on word-final consonant cluster simplification

Type of cluster	Preceding environment	Following environment	No. absent/ No. observed	Percent absent
M	Spirant	—##C	175/241	72.6
B	Spirant	—##C	33/59	55.9
M	Stop	—##C	8/15	53.3
B	Stop	—##C	17/58	29.3
M	Sonorant	—##C	30/62	*48.4
B	Sonorant	—##C	11/39	28.2
M	Spirant	—##	16/53	30.2
B	Spirant	—##	4/15	26.7
M	Stop	—##	1/4	25.0
B	Stop	—##	0/10	* 0.0
M	Sonorant	—##	2/13	15.4
B	Sonorant	—##	3/10	*30.0
M	Spirant	—##V	11/89	12.4
B	Spirant	—##V	10/29	*34.5
M	Sonorant	—##V	7/29	*24.1
B	Sonorant	—##V	1/36	2.8
M	Stop	—##V	0/0	0.0
B	Stop	—##V	0/0	0.0

out that the phonological status of [l] as +continuant or -continuant is somewhat of an undecided question; the exact phonological quality of [l] based on continuance is presently in a state of flux for most linguists:

> The characterization of the liquid [l] in terms of the continuant-noncontinuant scale is even more complicated. If the defining characteristic of the stop is taken (as above) as total blockage of air flow, then [l] must be viewed as a continuant and must be distinguished from [r] by the feature of 'laterality'. If, on the other hand, the defining characteristic of stops is taken to be blockage of air flow *past the primary stricture*, then [l] must be included among the stops. The phonological behavior of [l] in some languages supports somewhat the latter interpretation. As noted above (Section 4.7.2), in Chippewyan the lateral series parallels the nonlateral series if [l] is regarded as a continuant. Moreover, continuants (including [l]) are subject to voicing alternations which do not affect noncontinuants (Li 1946). On the other hand, there are other facts in different languages which suggest that [l] is best regarded as a noncontinuant (with the definition of the feature adjusted accordingly). Thus, for instance, in certain dialects of English spoken in Scotland, diphthongs are lax before noncontinuants and tense before continuants

(Lloyd 1908). Thus there is [r´ʌjd] but [ŕajz]. The liquids [l] and [r] pattern in parallel fashion, the former with the noncontinuants and the latter with the continuants: [t´ʌjl] but [ťajr]. (Chomsky and Halle 1968:318)

Based on Chomsky and Halle's analysis of [l], it was decided to consider [l] as -continuant. The North End data were then reanalyzed. The stop + stop clusters and sonorant + stop clusters of [ld] and [nd] were combined to form a new class called 'Sonorant + Stop' (abbreviated as S+S). This new class was characterized by the phonological feature -continuant as shown in Table 4.10.

Table 4.10. Cross products of potential constraints on word-final consonant cluster simplification

Type of cluster	Preceding environment	Following environment	No. absent/ No. observed	Percent absent
M	Spirant	__##C	175/241	72.6
B	Spirant	__##C	33/59	55.9
M	S+S	__##C	38/77	49.4
B	S+S	__##C	28/97	28.9
M	Spirant	__##	16/53	*30.2
B	Spirant	__##	4/15	26.7
M	S+S	__##	3/17	17.6
B	S+S	__##	3/20	15.0
M	Spirant	__##V	11/89	12.4
B	Spirant	__##V	10/29	*34.5
M	S+S	__##V	7/42	*16.7
B	S+S	__##V	1/83	1.2

As Table 4.10 shows, it was again impossible to establish a clear-cut, precise, and statistically symmetrical rank ordering of the preceding phonological constraints even by using a linguistic *deus ex machina* method of combining sonorants with stops under the linguistic rubric of -continuant. To produce a significant form of a variable rule, it is first necessary to establish a well-ordered hierarchy of constraints. The analysis of the preceding environment proved to be too inconclusive in determining with any significant degree of confidence the potential effect of the preceding consonants on cluster simplification. Therefore, it was decided to eliminate the three separate and specific categories of consonants and to refer to them simply as 'preceding consonants.' When this was done, a well-ordered hierarchy resulted. The cross product percentages for both monomorphemic and bimorphemic clusters with preceding consonants and following consonant, pause, or vowel are shown in Table 4.11.

Notice in Table 4.11 that the four highest percentages of simplification occur in the absence of a following vowel, that is, when a consonant or a pause follows

82 / The Italian-American child: His sociolinguistic acculturation

Table 4.11. Cross product percentages of two major constraints on word-final consonant cluster simplification in the speech of the Italian-American children

Preceding environment	Following environment	No. absent/ No. observed	Percent absent
C	##C	213/318	67.0
C#	##C	61/156	39.1
C	##	19/70	27.1
C#	##	7/35	20.0
C	##V	18/131	13.7
C#	##V	11/112	9.8

the word boundary. Of the six environments, the highest frequency is obtained when a consonant follows and the lowest when the following segment is a vowel. The results displayed in Table 4.11 indicate then that the most important constraint favoring simplification is the absence of a vowel following the cluster; the second most important constraint is the presence of a consonant. A third factor, the presence or absence of an intervening morpheme boundary, is also indicated in the table. In each case of combination with the other constraints, a morpheme boundary shows an inhibitory effect on simplification. For instance, when a consonant follows, there is a higher percentage of cluster simplification when no morpheme boundary intervenes (67.0 percent) than when one does (39.1 percent). The same is true in the case of a following utterance pause when an intervening morpheme boundary is absent (27.1 percent) than where an intervening morpheme boundary is present (20.0 percent). Again, the inhibitory effect is present when a vowel follows: 13.7 percent vs. 9.8 percent. Therefore, the absence of an intervening morpheme boundary constitutes the third most important constraint on simplification for the North End data.

Variable rule for word-final consonant cluster simplification. The hierarchy shown in Table 4.11 then provides for the assignment of alpha, beta, and gamma constraints on consonant cluster simplification as shown in the following variable rule.

$$[+\text{cons}] \rightarrow (\emptyset) \ / \ \Gamma \sim \begin{pmatrix} -\text{seg} \\ +\text{FB} \\ -\text{WB} \end{pmatrix} \underline{\qquad} \begin{bmatrix} -\text{seg} \\ -\text{FB} \\ +\text{WB} \end{bmatrix} \begin{bmatrix} A \sim \begin{pmatrix} +\text{voc} \\ -\text{cons} \end{pmatrix} \\ B \begin{pmatrix} -\text{voc} \\ +\text{cons} \end{pmatrix} \end{bmatrix}$$

Read: The final consonant appearing in a word-final consonant cluster becomes variably deleted in the environment of three hierarchically ranked constraints: the most highly favoring constraint is when the following word does not begin with a vowel; the second most favoring constraint is when the following word begins with a consonant (i.e., is not followed by a pause); and the third most favoring constraint is the absence of a preceding intervening morpheme boundary.

Correlations with Social Factors

The frequencies of word-final consonant cluster simplifications were correlated with the three familiar independent social variables of grade-age, sexual identity, and ethnicity as well as the two combined social variables of sexual identity and ethnicity, and grade-age and ethnicity. The analyses of these sociolinguistic correlations indicated that patterns with simplified clusters were highly similar to sociolinguistic patterns discovered in despirantized interdental fricatives.

Covariation with grade-age, sex, and ethnicity. The tabulations of the grade-age stratification for cluster simplification resulted once again in the familiar pattern that fourth graders had the highest frequency rate of socially stigmatized forms, the eighth graders the lowest, and the first graders an intermediate frequency. The fourth grade children simplified word-final consonant clusters 44.8 percent, eighth graders 34.8 percent, and the first graders 39.1 percent. Males continued to show a higher frequency rate (44.2 percent) than females (36.6 percent) when the sexual identity factor was studied in relationship to consonant clusters. However, in correlating ethnicity with consonant clusters, it was found that although bilingual speakers had a slightly higher frequency rate (41.0 percent) than monolingual speakers (39.0 percent), for all practical purposes, both sets of speakers could be considered as having the identical frequencies. Unlike the consistent patterns for lower frequencies of despirantizations among bilinguals and higher frequencies among monolinguals, the latter had a slightly lower frequency rate than bilinguals when consonant cluster simplifications were studied. The frequency rate figures for all three independent social variables in relation to cluster simplification are shown in Table 4.12.

Covariation with sex and ethnicity. The tabulated data for the combined social factors of sexual identity and ethnicity showed that monolingual females had the lowest frequencies of cluster simplifications (33.6 percent). Bilingual females, who consistently had the lowest despirantization rates, had the second lowest (39.3 percent), whereas both monolingual and bilingual males had the same percentage of cluster simplifications (43.5 percent).

Covariation with grade-age and ethnicity. Previous correlations with despirantization frequencies indicated the general pattern that fourth grade monolingual and bilingual speaker had generally the same frequency rates, but among both sets of speakers in the first and eighth grades, there was always a considerable difference in despirantized percentages. Bilinguals consistently had a lower rate of despirantizations than monolinguals. When the frequency rates of cluster

Table 4.12. Covariation of word-final consonant cluster simplifications in casual speech with grade-age, sex, and ethnicity

Grade-Age	No. absent/ No. observed	Percent absent
1	79/202	39.1
4	154/344	44.8
8	96/276	34.8
Total =	329/822	
Sex		
Males	164/371	44.2
Females	165/451	36.6
Total =	329/822	
Ethnicity		
Monolinguals	164/420	39.0
Bilinguals	165/402	41.0
Total =	329/822	

simplifications were studied in relation to grade-age and ethnicity, it was discovered that although the general pattern that fourth grade monolingual and bilingual speakers had very similar simplification percentages (monolinguals: 47.0 percent vs. bilinguals 42.7 percent), the eighth grade monolingual and bilingual speakers had almost identical scores, 34.0 percent and 35.7 percent respectively, whereas first grade monolinguals had 33.6 percent and bilinguals, 45.3 percent.

Narrative Reading Test

When the recorded reading passages (see appendix A) for each of the three grades were analyzed for the frequencies of word-final consonant cluster simplification, it was discovered that no 'true' consonant clusters could be found in either the first or fourth grade reading selections using Wolfram and Fasold's 'mixed voicing' caveat. The majority of potential clusters were eliminated due to mixed voicing of two or more consonants. A smaller number of potential clusters were eliminated because where a phonetic [t] or [d] was present, it was uncertain if the [t] or [d] segment represented the word-final cluster's last member [t]/[d] or the [t]/[d] of the following word (e.g. from *left to* right; *scanned the* first line). There was only one potential example of word-final consonant cluster in the fourth grade reading selection: the proper name, *Kern*, which appeared three times. This example was also eliminated because of the strong New England 'r-lessness' characteristic of dropping [r]. However, in the

4 Variable analysis of word-final consonant cluster simplification / 85

eighth grade selection, there were nine potential word-final consonant clusters. The number of potential clusters for the twenty eighth graders totalled 180. Of this number, only thirty-one (or 17.2 percent) were simplified. Males simplified more clusters (25.6 percent) than females (8.9 percent). Monolinguals tended to simplify clusters at a much higher rate (28.9 percent) than bilinguals (5.6 percent). Bilingual females simplified no clusters (0.0 percent) whereas monolingual females did so only four times (or 8.9 percent). Monlingual males had the highest number of simplifications, 22/45, (or 48.9 percent) and bilingual males had the next highest with 5/45 (or 11.1 percent).

The results of the analysis of the data culled from the informal or spontaneous conversations and from the formal reading selections, which was unfortunately limited only to the eighth grade reading passage, indicated that there was a frequency of simplifications of word-final consonant clusters in the informal speech style (40.0 percent) as compared to the more formal reading style (17.2 percent). The general patterns of the social variables grade-age and sexual identity were found again to be consistently systematic. Although the ethnicity factor in the informal style was practically identical (monolinguals: 39.0 percent vs. bilinguals: 41.0 percent), there was a considerable difference in the ethnicity factor when the formal reading style was analyzed (monolinguals: 28.9 percent vs. bilinguals: 5.6 percent). However, these differences cannot be taken too seriously since only thirty-one of 180 examples among twenty eighth graders were compared to 329 of 822 examples among all sixty informants.

Stylistic Variations

Since there were no minimal word-pairs for word-final consonant clusters, the careful reading style was necessarily eliminated for all three grades, both sexes, and both ethnic groups. Moreover, the eighth grade was the only grade whose reading selection contained any significant number of word-final consonant clusters. Therefore, the only possible comparison for stylistic variation according to grade-age, was that of the eighth grade, as Table 4.13 indicates.

In examining the data displayed in Table 4.13, it is clear that there is less consonant cluster simplification for the eighth graders' narrative reading style (17.2 percent) than in casual style (34.8 percent), and consequently, sexual identity and ethnicity correlations also reflect only the eighth graders, as shown in Table 4.13. There is the expected stratified decrease in narrative reading style when both sex and ethnicity were compared to both casual and narrative reading styles. Males had a decreased frequency rate from 44.2 percent to 25.6 percent; females had a decrease from 36.6 percent to 8.9 percent. Monolingual speakers decreased their frequency rate of word-final consonant cluster simplifications from 39.0 percent to 28.9 percent; and bilingual speakers from 41.0 percent to 5.6 percent. Unfortunately, the fact that there was an absence of narrative reading style for both the first and fourth grades made it impossible to compare and contrast all three styles with the three social variables. However, even with

Table 4.13. Covariation of word-final consonant cluster simplifications in casual, narrative reading, and careful reading styles with grade-age, sex, and ethnicity

Grade-Age	Casual	Narrative reading	Careful reading
1	39.1	X	X
4	44.8	X	X
8	34.8	17.2	X
Sex			
Males	44.2	25.6	X
Females	36.6	8.9	X
Ethnicity			
Monolinguals	39.0	28.9	X
Bilinguals	41.0	5.6	X

the small amount of data available for both casual and narrative reading styles for the eighth graders, it is evident that once again there is a pattern exemplifying a well-defined decrease in the frequencies of word-final consonant cluster simplifications for each of the three social variables as the style shifts from a casual to a narrative reading one.

Summary

In conclusion, then, we find that the analyzed North End data showed that word-final consonant clusters are variably simplified according to well-ordered hierarchical phonological constraints as indicated in the variable rule: the most important constraint favoring simplification is the absence of a following vowel; the second most important constraint is the presence of a following consonant; and the third most important constraint is the absence of an intervening morpheme boundary.

Extralinguistic correlations with cluster simplifications substantiated many of the sociolinguistic patterns already found in Chapter 3 in which the social variables of grade-age, sex, and ethnicity were studied. For example, when despirantization was correlated with the three basic social variables, it was discovered that fourth graders consistently had higher frequencies of socially stigmatized despirantization, while eighth graders had the lowest frequencies and first graders intermediate frequencies. When word-final consonant cluster simplifications were correlated with the same three basic social variables, once again the identical pattern resulted: fourth graders had the highest frequencies of cluster simplifications, eighth graders the lowest, and the first graders intermediate frequencies.

Furthermore, just as despirantization frequencies were higher among males than females, so cluster simplifications were higher among males than females. Finally, while despirantization frequencies were higher for monolinguals than bilinguals, cluster simplification frequencies were only slightly higher for bilinguals (41.0 percent) than for monolinguals (39.0 percent).

Finally, with respect to stylistic variations, just as there was a sharp decrease of despirantization frequencies from casual style to narrative reading style with the three basic social variables, there was also an identical decrease in cluster simplifications in these two styles for the three social variables with the exception of the narrative reading style for the first and fourth grades since no potential clusters appeared in these reading texts.

There are, therefore, strong tendencies in which covariation for word-final consonant cluster simplification and the social variables manifest systematically ordered patterns which are almost identical to the patterns of despirantization discussed in Chapter 3.

5
Variable Analysis of Third Person Singular Present Tense Verb Concord

General Remarks

The present tense in English is marked by the suffix -s only when the subject of the verb involved is third person singular. The Standard American English form of the verb, *eat*, for example, is *eats* if the subject is a singular noun or pronoun such as *he, she*, or *it*. The third person singular present tense verb concord suffix -s, or symbolized as Z_3 (Gleason 1961), has been shown by a number of linguists to be a socially diagnostic marker of language use among nonstandard speakers of English (Labov et al. 1968; Wolfram 1969, 1974; Fasold 1972). These linguists have demonstrated that speakers with the lowest scores on measurements of conventional social status have the highest percentages representing deleted Z_3 verb concord. In fact, the absence of Z_3 for many Black English speakers is so close to 100.0 percent that some linguists doubt that this suffix is part of the grammar of their spoken dialects at all (Labov et al. 1968:164; Wolfram 1969:137; Fasold 1972:146-147).

After examining the North End recorded data of the Italian-American children, it was found that the presence or absence of the third person singular verb suffix marker -s was reasonably easy to determine. Every potential instance of Z_3 verb concord was tabulated for all sixty informants, with the exception of those cases where a word beginning with a sibilant followed Z_3 as exemplified by the following sentences:

(1) My baby sister always *walks so* slow I hate to go out with her. (27)
(2) Sometimes my father *drives so* fast and I get real scared. (9)

These and similar examples of Z_3 were not tabulated because in so many instances the sibilant could not be satisfactorily distinguished phonetically, and as a result, it proved impossible to assign [s] to the following word alone or to both the following word and the putative Z_3 suffix. Thus, eliminating these ambiguous examples from the corpus, there remained 287 potential examples of

Z_3 and of this number the verb concord suffix -s was clearly absent in the speech of sixty North End children 20.6 percent (or 59/287).

Irregular Verbs

Fasold (1972:112-125) clearly explains that there are four irregular verbs with respect to Z_3 suffixation in Standard American English (other than modals) for which the third person singular present tense is not formed simply by the addition of the suffix marker -s. The four irregular verbs are: *have, do, say,* and *be.* The Z_3 form for *have* is *has,* not **haves;* for *do,* it is *does,* not **dos;* for *say,* it is *says* which is pronounced as [sɛz] , not [sɛɬz] ; and finally, for *be,* it is *is,* not **bes.* Since *be* has suppletive present tense forms which act differently from other verbs in English, Fasold's suggestion (1972:122-123) not to tabulate the present tense form *is* has been followed in this chapter.

Unlike speakers of nonstandard Black English whose speech reflects a strong tendency not to inflect *have* and *do,* the speech of the North End children does not manifest systematic variation of the verbs *have* and *do.* Of the twenty-six examples of *have* culled from the spontaneous conversations of the sixty informants, there were only six occurrences of noninflected *have,* some of which are exemplified by the following sentences:

(1) The house *have* three of them. (13)
(2) Then he *have* to count to one hundred. (16)
(3) Only the oldest one *have* to pay. (22)

Of the sixteen examples of *do* found in the North End data, only five examples manifested the noninflected form, for example:

(1) He *do*. (13)
(2) My baby sister sometimes *do* that. (16)

When Fasold (1972:123-124) investigated the irregular verb, *do,* he discovered that the presence of the contracted form of *not,* as in *don't* or *doesn't,* seemed to favor the absence of -s among his black informants. He found that the negative forms were used more often without -s than were the affirmative forms. The analysis of the North End data revealed the same linguistic phenomenon.

It should be noted that both *do* and *have* function as either auxiliary verbs or as main verbs, and that *don't* and *doesn't* function only when *do* is acting as an auxiliary. The North End data tend to substantiate Fasold's hypothesis (1972:123) that the presence of *not* may be irrelevant and that -s may be absent more often when the verb is serving as its auxiliary function. Fasold indicated that the positive forms of *do* used as main verbs show -s absence somewhat less frequently than when *do* is used as an auxiliary. The North End data, however, proved to be too scarce to prove conclusively that indeed this is also the case with the Italian-American children, since only five examples of *do* were extracted from the recorded data. Nevertheless, taking the paucity of examples of negative *do* into consideration, thirty-eight in number, there was more -s

90 / The Italian-American child: His sociolinguistic acculturation

absence with negative *do* forms than with regular verbs, again confirming what some previous studies on Z_3 have discovered (Fasold 1972:124).

The irregular verb, *say*, was also not tabulated in the Z_3 suffix absence data because this verb's irregular vowel shifts from present tense non-third person singular form of [se$'$] to present tense third person singular [sez]. Nevertheless, it is interesting to note that *say* had the highest frequency of Z_3 suffix absence when compared to Z_3 absence of *have* and *do*. As Table 5.1 indicates, the North End data revealed that Z_3 was absent 62.5 percent of the time.

Although neither Fasold (1972) in his Washington, D.C., study nor Wolfram (1974) in his New York City Puerto Rican study tabulated *have, do,* or *say* within their Z_3 absence data, Wolfram did compare the number of Z_3 absences of *have, do,* and *say* by a group of Puerto Rican adolescents with restricted black contacts. The North End Italian-American informants, who have had similar restricted cultural and linguistic contact with black speakers, showed compatible results with Wolfram's Puerto Rican informants, as Table 5.1 indicates.

Table 5.1. Comparison of Z_3 absence with irregular and regular verbs in the speech of New York City Puerto Rican adolescents and Boston's North End Italian-American children having restricted black contact

	Puerto Ricans			Italian-Americans		
	Intact	Absent	Total	Intact	Absent	Total
Have	29	12	41	20	6	26
Percent absent = 29.3				23.1		
Do	8	3	11	11	5	16
Percent absent = 27.3				31.3		
Don't	14	19	33	24	14	38
Percent absent = 57.6				36.8		
Say	41	31	72	9	15	24
Percent absent = 43.1				62.5		
Regular verbs	498	94	592	228	59	287
Percent absent = 15.9				20.6		
Irregular verbs						
Percent absent = 41.4				38.5		
Regular and irregular verbs						
Percent absent = 21.2				25.1		

Regular Verbs

Phonological environments. All possible phonological constraints on Z_3 absence were investigated. In Standard American English, the Z_3 suffix has three phonetic realizations: [s], [z], and [ɨz]. The factors determining which of these three phonetic alternants is to be used depend solely on the phonological features of the final segment of the base word. The [s] form occurs following nonstrident voiceless consonants; the [z] form follows nonstrident voiced consonants, including also all vowels; and the [ɨz] form follows all strident consonants.

Generally speaking, if Z_3 absence were due to phonological constraints, it is virtually certain that the bisegmental variant [ɨz] would show a significant difference in frequency rate from the [s] and [z] variants. To delete [ɨz], a phonological rule or series of rules would be needed to delete both the consonant [z] and the reduced vowel [ɨ]. For a phonological rule to delete [s] or [z], only a sibilant deletion rule would be needed. The data in Table 5.2 shows that Z_3 was absent 7.7 percent more often for [ɨz] than for [s] and [z] in all 287 examples of regular verb forms.

Since the results of the analyzed data for Z_3 absence indicated that there is a 7.7 percent difference between [ɨz] (27.8 percent) and [s], [z] (20.1 percent), there was a strong suspicion that the five instances of Z_3 deletion for [ɨz] might be due primarily to an interference factor on the part of the informants. This suspicion that linguistic interference was influencing Z_3 absence of [ɨz] was determined. Of the five [ɨz] deletions, two were made by Informant 8 (see appendix B), a six-year-old first grade bilingual female who had immigrated to Boston's North End less than two years before the time of research. Another two deletions were made by Informant 25, a ten year-old fourth grade bilingual male who had lived in Italy as a boy before coming to the North End three years previously. The final deletion of [ɨz] was made by Informant 26, a ten-year-old bilingual female who has lived in the North End only four years. Therefore, it was concluded that the uniquely higher frequencies for [ɨz] deletion were due to a heavy interference of Italian on the American English speech performance and not due to systematic variation.

Table 5.2. Comparison of the absence of [ɨz] and [s] or [z] representing Z_3 verb concord

	[ɨz]	[s] [z]
Present	13	215
Absent	5	54
Percent absent	27.8	20.1
N = 287		

Preceding environments. The first preceding environment was examined to see whether or not the preceding segment before Z_3 suffixation consisted in a single consonant or a double consonant. It was found that Z_3 was absent after single consonants 21.5 percent (or 31/144) and after double consonants 21.6 percent (or 16/74). The .1 percent differential between single and double consonants would absolutely rule out any potential phonological constraint on either a preceding single or double consonant.

The second preceding phonological environment was investigated in terms of determining whether or not the preceding segment of the base verb consisted in a consonant or a vowel. Z_3 was absent 17.4 percent (or 12/69) when a vowel preceded it whereas Z_3 was absent 21.6 percent or (47/218) when a consonant preceded it, as Table 5.3 indicates.

Table 5.3. Comparison of the effect of a preceding vowel and consonant on Z_3 deletion

	V __	C __
Present	57	171
Absent	12	47
Percent absent	17.4	21.5
N = 287		

The third likely preceding phonological constraint to be investigated was the possible effect of the voicing quality of all preceding consonants. It was found that when all preceding voiceless consonants were present, Z_3 was absent 23.9 percent (or 26/109) whereas when all preceding voiced consonants were present, Z_3 was absent 16.7 percent (or 15/90). Therefore, a very likely constraint seemed to be the preceding voiceless segments, as Table 5.4 shows.

Table 5.4. Comparison of the effect of preceding voiceless and voiced consonants on Z_3 deletion

	Cvl __	Cvd __
Present	83	75
Absent	26	15
Percent absent	23.9	16.7
N = 199		

Following environment. The effect of the following phonological environment was also investigated since one very likely constraint would be the effect of the following segment on Z_3; that is, whether or not a vowel, consonant, or utterance pause follows a word to which a Z_3 suffix is affixed. After the

5 Variable analysis of third person singular present tense verb concord / 93

following environments were analyzed, it was found that a following vowel favored deletion 13.2 percent and a consonant favored deletion 22.5 percent, and utterance pause 38.9 percent, as shown in Table 5.5.

Table 5.5. Comparison of the effect of a following vowel, consonant, and utterance pause on Z_3 deletion

	___##V	___##C	___##
Present	79	138	11
Absent	12	40	7
Percent absent	13.2	22.5	38.9

N = 287

X^2 = 37.04   p. < .001

Since it is evident from the data presented in Table 5.5 that a following nonsegment favored deletion of the -s suffix for third person singular present tense, a following nonsegment was considered a likely candidate as a potential constraint. Furthermore, if the Z_3 suffixes are deletable by phonological rules operating on the phonetic verb concord markers [s], [z], and [ɨz], we would expect that the surrounding phonological environments would be a crucial factor in determining the appropriate constraints since such constraints tend to operate hierarchically. Also, if the constraints were hierarchically ordered, we would expect one environment to be ranked over the other.

Determining the hierarchy of constraints. It now remains to determine the hierarchy of constraints for the deletion of third person singular present tense of regular verbs. The cross product percentages for the preceding and following environments are displayed in Table 5.6.

Table 5.6. Cross products of potential constraints on Z_3 deletion

Preceding environment	Following environment	No. deleted/ No. observed	Percent deleted
Cvl	___##	2/5	40.0
V	___##	2/6	*33.3
Cvd	___##	3/7	*42.9
Cvl	___##C	17/66	25.8
V	___##C	12/54	22.2
Cvd	___##C	11/58	19.0
Cvl	___##V	7/38	18.4
V	___##V	4/28	14.3
Cvd	___##V	1/25	4.0

Notice in Table 5.6 that the highest percentages for Z_3 deletion occur in the absence of a following segment, that is, when only an utterance pause is present without either a vowel or consonant. Note, however, that there are two percentages marked by an asterisk (33.3 and 42.9 percents), which indicate these percentages are out of order within the hierarchy. These two percentages do not fit within the neat descending hierarchical rank-ordering so familiar with variable rule theory. Nevertheless, these minor deviations within the hierarchy were excused based on the North End data's paucity of examples (2/6 and 3/7) for utterance pause following Z_3. Therefore, with all nine hierarchically ordered preceding and following potential constraints shown in Table 5.6, the following form of the variable rule can be written as:

$$\begin{bmatrix} +\text{cons} \\ +\text{cont} \end{bmatrix} \rightarrow (\emptyset) / \Gamma \sim \begin{bmatrix} +\text{voi} \\ \Delta \, (+\text{nuc}) \end{bmatrix} \quad \#\underline{\quad}\#\# \quad A \sim \left(\begin{bmatrix} +\text{seg} \\ B \, (+\text{cons}) \end{bmatrix} \right)$$

Read: Third person singular present tense verb suffix -s becomes variably deleted in the environment of four hierarchically ranked constraints: the most highly favoring constraint is the absence of a following segment (i.e. the presence of an utterance pause); if, however, a segment does indeed follow, then the second most favoring constraint is the presence of a consonantal segment; the third most favoring constraint is the absence of voicing in the preceding segment; but if the preceding segment is indeed voiced, then the fourth most favoring constraint is when that voiced segment is a vowel.

Note in the above variable rule that Z_3 suffix marker -s was written with the phonological features +consonant and +continuant, thus distinguishing -s suffix marker from past tense marker which is +consonant and −continuant. Also note that several peculiarities are found in the above variable rule. First, as the cross products indicate in Table 5.6, the highest percentages or alpha constraint refer to the presence of a following nonsegment, that is, if no vowel or consonant follows but merely an utterance pause, then deletion of Z_3 is promoted. However, if there is no utterance pause, and therefore, some kind of segment does follow, necessarily either a vowel or consonant, then Z_3 is promoted when the following segment is a consonant and not a vowel. Thus, the beta constraint was assigned to the following consonant when and only when a segment follows Z_3.

A similar situation occurs with the preceding constraints. It is surprising that the North End data revealed the fact that the feature voicing (i.e. voiced or voiceless) of the preceding segment outranks the consonant vs. vowel dichotomy which is the expected phonological dichotomy. However, from the data displayed in Table 5.6, voicing is apparently the stronger constraint because vowels are intermediate between voiceless consonants and voiced consonants. Since this is a surprising outcome from the analysis of the North End data of 287 examples, it would be most important for validation purposes to replicate this Z_3 research with other North End grade school children. Nevertheless, there is the definite possibility that preceding vowels are not really a constraint at all, but rather voicing is the true constraint. Both the gamma and delta constraints in the above form of the variable rule reflect this surprising phonological phenomenon in that the gamma constraint is the absence of voiced segments (+voi), and the delta constraint (+nuc) is the presence of vowels (which are obviously always voiced) when and only when the preceding segment happens to be voiced. That is, if the preceding segment happens to be voiced (and therefore the gamma constraint of voiceless consonants is necessarily absent), then of the two possible voiced constraints, vowels and voiced consonants, the delta constraint would necessarily be vowels (+nuc).

Since there is the definite possibility that preceding vowels alone are not a true constraint, the same data in Table 5.6 were reanalyzed in terms of preceding voiced and voiceless segments. As a result of this voicing criterion, the two classes of preceding vowels and voiced consonants were collapsed into the one class of preceding 'voiced segments' and voiceless consonants remained as the class of preceding 'voiceless segments.' Therefore, the data displayed in Table 5.7 indicate that the preceding potential constraints are now voiced and voiceless segments and the following potential constraints remain as utterance pause, consonant, and vowel.

Table 5.7. Cross products of potential constraints on Z_3 deletion

Preceding environment	Following environment	No. deleted/ No. observed	Percent deleted
Voiceless	__ ##	2/5	40.0
Voiced	__ ##	5/13	38.5
Voiceless	__ ##C	17/66	25.8
Voiced	__ ##C	23/112	20.5
Voiceless	__ ##V	7/38	18.4
Voiced	__ ##V	5/53	9.4

Notice in Table 5.7 that the two highest percentages once again reflect the situation where the following constraint is an utterance pause or the absence of a segment. The next two highest percentages reflect the presence of a following consonant. The remaining two percentages reflect the presence of a following vowel. In each case of correlation with the following potential constraints, there is an inhibitory effect of the preceding voiced segment. For instance, when an utterance pause follows, there is a higher percentage of Z_3 deletion (40.0 percent) when no voiced segment precedes Z_3 than when one does (38.5 percent). The same is true when no voiced segment precedes and there is a following consonant (25.8 percent) as compared to when a voiced segment precedes and a consonant follows (20.5 percent). Therefore, the absence of a preceding voiced segment (or the presence of a voiceless segment) promotes Z_3 deletion, and in this case, voicelessness is the gamma constraint.

Variable rule for Z_3 deletion. Therefore, based on the data displayed in Table 5.7, the form of the variable rule for deletion of the third person singular present tense of regular verbs can be written as:

$$\begin{bmatrix} +\text{cons} \\ +\text{cont} \end{bmatrix} \rightarrow (\emptyset) \ / \ [\Gamma(-\text{voi})] \ \#\_\_\#\# \ A \sim \left(\begin{bmatrix} +\text{seg} \\ B \ (+\text{cons}) \end{bmatrix} \right)$$

> Read: Third person singular present tense verb suffix -s becomes variably deleted in the environment of three hierarchically ranked constraints: the most highly favoring constraint is the absence of a following segment (i.e. the presence of utterance pause); the second most favoring constraint is the presence of a following consonant; and the third most favoring constraint is the presence of a preceding voiceless segment.

As in the Z_3 deletion variable rule based on the data presented in Table 5.6, the alpha and beta constraints in the above variable rule indicate that the absence of a following segment [+seg] is the most favorable (alpha) constraint; yet, if, and when and only when, a following segment is present, then of either of the two possibilities, a following vowel or a following consonant, it will be a following consonant (+cons) that will be the next strongest favoring (beta) constraint. The constraint which is the next most favorable for Z_3 deletion is the gamma constraint, which is now simply preceding voicelessness or the absence of voiced segments (-voi) which necessarily includes both vowels and voiced consonants.

Correlations with Social Factors

The frequencies of Z_3 deletion were consequently correlated with the three social variables, grade-age, sexual identity, and ethnicity, and then with the two combined social variables of sexual identity and ethnicity, and grade-age and ethnicity. Once again the sociolinguistic correlations found in the North End data for Z_3 deletion were generally the same systematic patterns found in Chapters 3 and 4.

Covariation with grade-age, sex, and ethnicity. The tabulated data for the grade-age social variable indicated that the fourth graders had the highest Z_3 deletion rate (30.7 percent) of either the eighth graders (14.5 percent) or the first graders (15.4 percent). Unlike previous observations made with grade-age stratification regarding both interdental fricatives and consonant cluster simplification, there was not a large percentage differential of Z_3 deletion (15.4 percent vs. 14.5 percent). However, the sexual identity factor continued to show its marked characteristic in that males deleted more Z_3 (24.6 percent) than females (17.0 percent). But when ethnicity was correlated with the number of Z_3 deletions, it was found that the monolinguals had a lower frequency level of Z_3 deletion (16.4 percent) than bilinguals (25.8 percent). The frequency rate figures for all three independent social variables for Z_3 deletion are shown in Table 5.8.

Table 5.8. Covariation of Z_3 deletion in casual speech with grade-age, sex, and ethnicity

Grade-Age	No deleted/ No. observed	Percent deleted
1	18/117	15.4
4	31/101	30.7
8	10/69	14.5
Total =	59/287	
Sex		
Males	33/134	24.6
Females	26/153	17.0
Total =	59/287	
Ethnicity		
Monolinguals	26/159	16.4
Bilinguals	33/128	25.8
Total =	59/287	

Covariation with sex and ethnicity. The tabulated data for the combined social factors of sexual identity and ethnicity showed the monolingual females had the lowest frequencies of Z_3 deletion (12.1 percent). Bilingual females had the second lowest frequencies (19.5 percent) whereas both monolingual males (24.2 percent) and bilingual males (31.6 percent) had higher frequencies of Z_3 deletion.

Covariation with grade-age and ethnicity. When the combined social variables of grade-age and ethnicity were studied in relationship to the frequencies of Z_3 deletion, it was noted that although the fourth grade monolinguals and bilinguals were fairly close in frequencies (monolinguals: 32.1 percent vs. bilinguals: 28.9 percent), fourth grade bilinguals had a slightly lower rate than fourth grade monolinguals. This was not the case, however, among both sets of informants in the first and eighth grades. In these latter grades, monolinguals consistently had lower frequencies that bilinguals: first grade monolinguals, 14.3 percent; bilinguals, 19.2 percent; eighth grade monolinguals, 10.9 percent; bilinguals, 17.1 percent.

Narrative Reading Test

Of the three reading selections (see appendix A) for each of the appropriate grade levels, the first grade reading did not contain any Z_3 verb concord suffixation. In the fourth grade reading selection, however, there were two sentences in which examples of Z_3 were present:

(1) Mrs. Kern *bakes* everything herself in the kitchen of their home behind the store.
(2) Children in the neighborhood like to go to the bakery for their mothers, for Mrs. Kern always *gives* them a cookie.

When the recorded reading selections for the fourth grade were analyzed for the frequencies of Z_3 deletion for the two examples, *bakes* and *gives*, it was discovered that there was a deletion rate of only 12.5 percent (or 5/40). Of the five deletions of Z_3, one was made by a fourth grade bilingual female and the remaining four were made by monolingual females.

In the eighth grade reading selection, there were eight examples of Z_3: *changes* (appeared three times), *starts* (appeared twice), *comes, jumps,* and *moves.* When each of the twenty eighth grade recordings were analyzed for all eight examples of Z_3, no deletions were noted for any of the 160 Z_3 realizations.

Stylistic Variations

There were no minimal word-pairs exemplifying the presence or absence of Z_3. Therefore, careful reading style was necessarily eliminated from any stylistic comparisons. Also, Z_3 did not appear in the first grade narrative reading selection so as a result, in Table 5.9, the cell marked *first grade* plus *narrative reading style* is vacated. It is important to recall that as noted in detail in the previous section on the narrative reading test, there were only two examples of Z_3 in the fourth grade reading passage. Of the forty possible realizations of Z_3, five were deleted. In the eighth grade passage, there were eight examples of Z_3, thus making the total number of Z_3 occurrences 160. But there were no deletions of Z_3 among any of the narrative reading recitations by eighth graders. Thus, the percentages under the narrative reading style heading need to be understood in light of the very limited number of examples of Z_3 in the texts.

When grade-age and sexual identity were compared to the number of Z_3 absences in both casual and narrative reading styles, there was a decrease in the number of Z_3 deletions when there was a shift in style from a casual to a narrative reading one. However, when ethnicity was investigated with respect to the two styles, there was an increase in Z_3 deletions for monolingual speakers, but this anomaly can be explained by the paucity of examples of Z_3 in both the fourth and eighth grade reading selections. Nevertheless, the data indicated in general that there was once again a decrease in the frequency of Z_3 deletions as the North End children shifted from casual style to narrative reading style.

Summary

In conclusion, then, the North End data revealed that Z_3 deletion in the speech of the Italian-American children of the North End is governed by a phonological rule. However, the analysis of Z_3 found in the literature on Black English is that the absence of the -s marker is due to syntactic processes rather

Table 5.9. Covariation of Z_3 deletion in casual, narrative reading, and careful reading styles with grade-age, sex, and ethnicity

Grade-Age	Casual	Narrative reading	Careful reading
1	15.4	X	X
4	30.7	X	X
8	14.5	X	X
Sex			
Males	24.6	00.0	X
Females	17.0	12.5	X
Ethnicity			
Monolinguals	16.4	80.0	X
Bilinguals	25.0	20.0	X

than phonological ones. There is much evidence for this conclusion given in Labov et al. (1968), Wolfram (1969, 1974), and Fasold (1970, 1972). The data in Black English found by all three linguists indicate that the observed frequencies of Z_3 absence reflect a sensitivity to syntactic factors rather than phonological factors as the North End data revealed. The phonological variable rule for the North End data indicated a number of hierarchically ordered constraints. Furthermore, the fact that fourth graders rarely deleted Z_3 in their reading selections and that no one in the eighth grade omitted a single example of Z_3 confirms the data of 287 examples that Z_3 absence is governed by a phonological variable rule in the speech of the Italian-American children.

Also, the sociolinguistic correlations with Z_3 exhibited the same patterns found for despirantization and word-final consonant cluster simplification. Fourth graders had the highest frequencies of socially stigmatized Z_3 absence, eighth graders the lowest, and first graders once again had intermediate frequencies. When sexual identity was correlated with Z_3 absence, males again had much higher frequencies of Z_3 absence than females. Although bilinguals had a lower rate of despirantization and only a slightly higher rate of cluster simplification than monolinguals, when ethnicity was compared with Z_3 absence, it was discovered that bilinguals had a higher frequency of Z_3 absences than monolinguals.

The data for Z_3 not only indicated that Z_3 absence is governed by a phonological rule, but they also tend to confirm the presence of sociolinguistic patterns similar to those found for despirantization and word-final consonant cluster simplification discussed in Chapters 3 and 4, respectively. It has become gradually evident in this discussion of the three linguistic variables that the North End children are quite sensitive to nonlinguistic social variables with respect to the three linguistic phenomena of despirantization of interdental fricatives, word-final consonant cluster simplification, and Z_3 absence.

6
Language Maintenance and Language Shift in the North End

General Remarks

In the geographically isolated area of Boston's North End, there are two linguistically distinct speech communities which are in contact with one another: Italian and English. The continually felt presence and strong influence of Italian in this area are due partially to the small but constant influx of newly arrived immigrant families from southern Italy who come to these shores under the sponsorship of a brother, sister, or close relative already established in the United States. English is also spoken in the North End, generally by second, third, and fourth generation Italian-Americans who for one reason or another have decided to continue living in the area. Joshua A. Fishman (1972:76) described linguistic situations similar to that of the North End as situations of language maintenance and language shift. These are concerned with 'the relationship between change (or stability) in language usage patterns, on the one hand, and ongoing psychological, social, or cultural processes, on the other hand, in populations that utilize more than one speech variety for intra-group or for inter-group purposes.' Moreover, Fishman maintains that it is not a rare situation at all for languages or variants of a language which are in contact with one another to displace each other among some speakers. This displacement of another language takes place especially when communication is carried on in interpersonal domains of language behavior.

Thus, the purpose of this chapter is to describe the nature and degree of maintenance by the Italian-American bilingual children as well as to describe what type of children reflect particular domains of language behavior, and under what conditions and to what degree do they maintain one language or shift from one language to the other. Fishman believes that the principal concern for sociolinguistics-minded researchers of language maintenance and language shift should be '*not* with interference phenomena per se but, rather, degrees of maintenance or displacement in conjunction with several sources and domains of variance in language behavior' (1972:76-77). Moreover, we have followed Fishman's suggestion to be eclectic regarding a number of possible approaches used by various disciplines studying language maintenance and shift. Since the study of language maintenance and shift is not under the exclusive domain of any one discipline—linguistics, sociology, psychology, anthropology—it seemed best that a combination of methodologies would be necessary to study and measure adequately the type of maintenance and shift currently existing in the North End. Thus, attempts were made in the original period of data gathering in the North End and subsequently in analyzing the data, to explore the current trends, status, and extent of language maintenance efforts in the North End.

The principal method of gathering the necessary data to define as accurately as possible the psychological, social, and cultural situation of maintaining Italian or switching from Italian to English was carried out by indepth interviews with each informant: three questionnaries[5] administered in a conversational manner; interviews with all three grade school principals and all teachers of the first, fourth, and eighth grades; interviews with pastors and priests of local churches, as well as with civic leaders and representatives of various social agencies, including community action program leaders. The 1970 Census reports for the North End area were also useful in understanding in a broader scope the change and stability of Italian in the North End. The particular means used for gathering the necessary data were decided upon as the best ones available at the time and under the given circumstances. Attention was given to spoken language and secondarily to read language according to Fishman's 'media variance' criteria (1972:79). Furthermore, for Fishman's 'locational or situational variance' model, it was decided that three styles should be analyzed for language maintenance and language shift: familial or intimate, informal, and formal. Finally, Fishman's model of 'domains' of language behavior in relationship to language maintenance and language shift was delimited to three language domains: the extent of comprehension and usage of Italian or English:

(1) with family members, including primarily the child's parents and siblings, and secondarily his close relatives such as grandparents, aunts, uncles, and cousins;
(2) with teachers and school administrators, and with other grade-age students within the school environment;
(3) with peers within the street, playground, or park environment.

Therefore, with the various measurements of language maintenance and shift, the language attitudes and behavior of the North End 'coordinately' bilingual and of the monolingual children were studied and analyzed. In summary, the two basic but dovetailing comprehensive questions that have guided my research, though very limited in comparison to the broad array of potential questions meriting serious examination of the North End, were the following:

(1) In what sociological context does the need for maintaining or shifting from Italian to English arise?
(2) What are the discernible psychological, social, and cultural variables, conditions, or factors motivating such maintenance of shift among the North End Italian-American bilingual children?

Fishman's challenging exhortation to uncover any significant influencing variables of language maintenance or shift motivated my desire to discover any significant psychological, social, and cultural variables.

> Underlying (or overlying) psychological, social and cultural *processes* are less fully listed or discussed by any of the above scholars than are demographic *groupings* or institutional *categories* per se. The result of such reliance on disjointed categories has been that no broadly applicable or dynamic theories, concepts or findings have been derived from most earlier studies. Indeed, the study of language maintenance and language shift currently lacks either a close relationship to theories of sociocultural change more generally or to theories of intergroup relations more specifically. Just as an understanding of socio-behavior-through-language must depend upon a general theory of society so the understanding of language maintenance or language shift must depend on a theory of socioculture contact and sociocultural change. (1972:94)

Italian-American children in the North End community. The population of the United States today derives from immigrants from many countries throughout the world. Those whose families came to our shores three and four generations ago from northern Europe are now often thought of as 'native' Americans; those whose families came more recently within the last sixty years from such countries, for example, as Germany, Greece, Poland, Hungary, Italy, China, and Japan, are more often considered 'ethnic minorities.' The mass immigration of over thirty million persons representing over sixty ethnic groups lasted from 1880 to 1920 (Hansen 1948). The Immigration Act of 1924 halted the influx of immigrants and established a quota system which limited the number of immigrants from any one country. But during that period of forty years, immigrants generally located themselves in cities and towns where their families and friends had previously immigrated and settled.

An ethnic group can be described as a community consisting of those who conceive of themselves as being alike because of their shared cultural heritage and who are so thought of by others. Like any ethnic group, the Italians in Boston's North End have a subordinate role in the larger, dominant American society in which Italians work and live. The newly arrived Italian immigrant to the North End must sooner or later learn the ways of the already acculturated second and third generation English-speaking Italian-Americans. This latter group are the dominant group numerically and politically in the North End. The term acculturation refers to the process of acquiring the culture of another ethnic group. Acculturation for immigrant southern Italians consists in becoming americanized to the ideological and value systems (Smith 1973a) exemplified in any number of financial, civic, and cultural ways in the Boston area. The adaptation of any ethnic group to American culture depends on various factors such as the age, sex, educational level, socioeconomic status, and of course, personality of the immigrant. Immigrant parents in the North End do not adapt to the socialization process as easily and quickly as their children for a number of reasons: age (immigrant parents have been accustomed to established life-styles, attitudes, and cultural norms); language (being older, many immigrant parents find learning English an arduous and lengthy task); educational level (the majority of mothers and fathers of immigrant children have no more than a fifth grade level education).

Furthermore, like any ethnic group immigrating to the United States, Italians must sooner or later come to grips with how different they think and feel themselves to be now that they are living in the United States; and the degree of cohesion with already established immigrants and with other newly arrived immigrant families.

There are a number of social variables influencing an ethnic group like the Italians in the North End. The socialization process for immigrants, especially the children of immigrant parents, presents certain definable characteristic patterns. There have been various studies which indicate that minority-group children are well aware of their distinct social status by the time they are five or six years old, although they are too inexperienced to understand the abstract meanings of such social status differentiations. In a study of four-year-old black and white children in New England, Mary Ellen Goodman (1952) discovered in her subjects not only the presence of race awareness but also race prejudice. Another study indicated that when compared with other nonethnic children, minority-group children 'show earlier and greater differentiation of their own group as well as more personal involvement in the group identification' (Yarrow 1958).

Second generation bilingual children, who were either born in Italy and then came to the North End with their immigrant parents or born in the North End of newly arrived immigrant parents, learn to develop two cultures and identities: those of the Italian ethnic community and those of the American national society. A bilingual child learns his Italian ethnic culture and identity primarily through his interactions with his family and relatives; his family's particular life-styles of eating, working, and recreating; hearing stories of family experiences; in general, the family's participation in the strong Italian community's way of life in the North End. However, Italian-speaking children also learn their culture in a sociologically modified form; a form whose strong constraints are determined principally by the social and cultural patterns of the geographical location in which they find themselves (Smith 1972a). Hence, immigrant children must learn how to cope with the social and cultural factors within the North End, a neighborhood within the city of Boston. The acculturating Italian immigrant family is quite different from typical Italian families in southern Italy. Because of the many differences immigrant parents quickly find when they come to live in the North End, misunderstandings, conflicts, frustrations, and a lack of openness in communicating thoughts and feelings inevitably develop in varying degrees between slowly acculturating Italian immigrant parents and their quickly acculturating children. Italian parents with their traditional set of ideological and value systems are often irritated at the attitudes and behavior of their children, and the latter, in turn, resent many of the restricting and 'old-fashioned' ideas and attitudes of their parents.

Since immigrant parents are unable to fall back on the cultural and social systems they were once accustomed to rely on in order to support their position, they are constantly being reminded, not only by their children, but also by the subtleties of the mass media and by the less subtle demands of the youth culture, that they as parents must attempt major adaptations. Erik Erikson (1963:160-161) points out that in these situations of conflicts of interests and ideas, ethnic children tend not to 'confirm' their parents. The life-style which their parents hold out as good and worthy does not represent a vital promise for the future for many ethnic children as they see it. Robert K. Merton (1968:281) indicates that what is happening among second generation ethnic children is that they change their 'reference groups.' A reference group is any group by whose standards one judges one's behavior. Some North End bilingual children no longer regard their parents or their inherited culture as a suitable reference group. As many bilingual children become more and more accustomed to the American way of life, they must necessarily judge themselves by the standards of their American monolingual peers, because, of course, they are being appraised and judged by them in school and on the streets and playgrounds.

Therefore, an Italian bilingual child has two statuses: his Italian ethnic status and his American status. As an Italian, he may be proud of his national heritage, culture, and Roman Catholic religion, but as an American, he may also be embarrassed or ashamed of his parents' strong Italian accent when they attempt to speak English, or angry at his parents' overly protective and harsh constraints on his social life. North End bilingual children live on the margins of two distinct cultures; they have loyalties to both, but they are not completely participant in either. As Shibutani and Kwan observe:

> Many of the problems confronting such individuals arise from their having to perform for two different and incongruous reference groups. Since contradictory demands are made upon them by the two audiences, they experience inner conflicts. When a man lives in two social worlds, each of which is a moral order, he cannot live up to all of his obligations. Where standards are inconsistent, he will be wrong in the eyes of one of the groups no matter what he does. He may be plagued by a sense of guilt even when he has done his very best. Some persons sometimes have difficulty developing a consistent self-conception. As Cooley pointed out, a man comes to conceive of himself as a particular kind of human being in response to the manner in which others treat him. But what happens to a man who looks simultaneously into two mirrors and sees sharply different images of himself? (1965:357)

Stratificational patterns of language maintenance and shift. The questionnaires (see appendix A), which were administered to all sixty informants, and the data culled from available school records were the primary sources of information for the subsequent covariations for language maintenance and shift in the North End. The following eight covariations were the results of this analysis:

(1) Covariation of bilingual children's use of Italian according to their *grade-age* and *sex*.
(2) Covariation of bilingual children's use of Italian according to their relationship with their *parents*.
(3) Covariation of bilingual children's use of Italian according to their relationship with their *siblings*.
(4) Covariation of bilingual children's use of Italian according to their relationship with their *relatives*.
(5) Covariation of bilingual children's use of Italian according to their relationship with their *peers*.
(6) Covariation of bilinguals children's use of Italian according to their relationship with their *teachers*.
(7) Covariation of *bilingual* children's attitudes toward *Italian* as a language and toward the *North End* as an ethnic neighborhood.
(8) Covariation of *monolingual* children's attitudes toward *Italian* as a language and toward the *North End* as an ethnic neighborhood.

Covariation of bilingual children's use of Italian according to grade-age and sex. Although all (100.0 percent) thirty bilingual informants were fully able to understand spoken Italian and to speak Italian fluently, only eleven bilingual children (or 36.7 percent) were found capable of reading Italian, and only elementary Italian as written in storybooks or comic books. Of the eleven who were capable of reading such basic Italian, four were in the first grade, two were in the fourth, and five were in the eighth grade. Furthermore, only four bilingual children (all eighth grade females) responded that they could write Italian, which consisted in elementary correspondence-type written prose to relatives in Italy. Since all thirty bilingual informants were randomly selected on the basis of their ability to communicate in both Italian and English, the proportion of males comprehending and speaking Italian was necessarily equal to that of females: 50.0 percent were males (or 15/30) and 50.0 percent were females (or 15/30).

Covariation of bilingual children's use of Italian according to their relationship with their parents. Although all bilingual children almost always communicated with their parents in Italian within the home (even under emotional stress situations as when being punished), some parents (30.0 percent) also wanted their children to speak English occasionally with them within the home so that they could learn a few necessary phrases in English for shopping purposes outside the North End area. In fact, slightly more mothers (83.3 percent) than fathers (76.7 percent) wished to learn English. Furthermore, parents wanted their children to learn English (96.7 percent), and hardly any parents (3.3 percent) thought their children should totally forget Italian as soon as possible. The majority of parents (93.3 percent) actually encouraged their children to continue learning and speaking Italian. It did not make a great deal of difference whether the speech setting was within the home, outside the home in the neighborhood shops, or even in the downtown shopping district; bilingual children (96.7 percent) felt comfortable speaking Italian to their parents even though they might have been overheard by non-Italians. There were no immigrant parents who could speak to their children either in fluent English or in half-English and half-Italian, although they would sometimes substitute common English words or phrases as *ice cream* and *O.K.* Therefore, although the majority of immigrant parents wanted their children to learn English in order to understand, speak, read, and write it for socioeconomic reasons, they have made it clear to their children that they are to maintain Italian as the medium of communication with them in their parent-child relationship. The respective roles of parent and child reflected the intimate speech style of Italian maintained within the tightly knit family structure so common in the North End.

Thus, there were no discernible data to indicate that either immigrant parents or their children have shifted from Italian to English. It is quite unlikely that English will displace Italian in the parent-child relationship. However, there was definitely a strong desire among immigrant parents to learn a modicum of English for practical purposes such as when purchasing merchandise, asking for information, or understanding television broadcasts. There was an extremely strong desire on the part of parents that their children learn English very well while at the same time holding on firmly to Italian.

Covariation of bilingual children's use of Italian according to their relationship with their siblings. Of all thirty bilinguals, 70.0 percent responded positively to the question regarding whether their parents wanted them to speak Italian with their brothers and sisters. The bilinguals who generally spoke Italian with their siblings ranged from 85.0 percent among first graders to 75.0 percent among fourth graders, and 45.0 percent among eighth graders. The speech settings in which siblings communicated with one another in Italian were almost always when they were alone with one another inside or outside their home, but seldom when any monolinguals were present. Even when siblings would argue with one another or would be under similar emotionally strained situations, they would speak in Italian with one another 70.0 percent of the time. Thus, the language maintenance and shift data show that the only clear option which exists for a bilingual child with regard to the domain of the immediate family is one between his parents and his siblings. For all practical purposes, a bilingual always communicates with his parents in Italian irrespective of the location or the presence of monolingual children or adults; whereas although he generally speaks Italian with his siblings within the home or out on the street, he seldom speaks Italian when monolinguals are present.

Covariation of bilingual children's use of Italian according to their relationship with their relatives. The study of language maintenance and shift regarding close relatives indicated that Italian is an extremely stable medium of communication for bilingual children (100.0 percent) when conversing with other relatives. However, Italian was shown to be less stable (76.7 percent) when bilingual cousins would come to visit a bilingual's home. Italian was drastically reduced (26.7 percent) when bilingual children and their bilingual cousins would leave the house and go out to play in the streets with monolingual children. Thus, bilingual children maintain Italian to a high degree with older relatives, but they gradually shift from Italian to English with bilingual cousins when Italian is spoken within the home and no monolinguals are present, in contrast to when bilinguals and their cousins leave the house and play with monolingual children. As a corollary, Italian is not only maintained to a high degree with parents, siblings, and close relatives who are adults, but it is also maintained to a very high degree (83.3 percent) with local shopkeepers when bilingual children are sent by their parents to deal with them.

Covariation of bilingual children's use of Italian according to their relationship with their peers. While all thirty bilingual children (100.0 percent) had some best friends who could understand and speak Italian, English was necessarily chosen as the language when bilingual children played with monolingual children, since monolinguals do not understand or speak Italian except for a small number of well-known set phrases such as *grazie, va bene, vai via*, and so on. When bilingual children interacted with other bilingual children within the home, at school recess, in the streets, or on the playground, then Italian was used 53.3 percent of the time. There were only twelve bilinguals (or 40.0 percent) who responded positively to question 24 regarding personal embarrassment when monolingual children overheard them speaking Italian either with adults or with other bilingual children. Of the twelve, six males and six females, four were in the first grade, seven in the fourth, and one in the eighth. Therefore, bilingual children tend to maintain Italian when speaking with other Italian-speaking children in the North End, but they quickly switch to English when the group suddenly becomes a mixture of both bilingual and monolingual children.

Covariation of bilingual children's use of Italian according to their relationship with their teachers. Although all thirty bilingual children admitted that they wished they could study Italian formally as a language in school, and twenty-one children (70.0 percent) thought it would be a good idea if teachers who were capable of speaking Italian would also teach part of the school day in Italian, the data culled from the research at the three schools showed that only one of the nine teachers for the first, fourth, and eighth grades was a bilingual speaker. All remaining eight teachers were of non-Italian descent and had no knowledge of Italian, although over 89.0 percent of the population is of Italian descent and the vast majority of this same population can at least understand spoken Italian.

The classroom is obviously a more formal speech setting than either the intimate familial environment of the bilingual's home, or the informal environment of peer groups on the streets or playgrounds. All thirty bilingual children found it necessary to speak in English within the classroom, except in those situations when a teacher asked a bilingual child to translate a point of instruction or request to a newly arrived immigrant child who, because of almost no understanding or speaking ability of English, is generally bewildered during history, religion, and social science presentations. However, teachers indicated in their interviews that newly arrived immigrant children show a surprising degree of comprehension when mathematics is taught with the aid of the blackboard. Presumably since mathematics is usually taught in methodological stratified lessons in which a great deal of clarifying information is not as necessary as it is when describing an event in history, religion, or English literature, immigrant children are able to grasp more quickly the essence of a teacher's presentation.

Covariation of bilingual children's attitudes toward Italian as a language and toward the North End as an ethnic neighborhood. The attitudes of bilingual children to the Italian language and the cultural milieu of the North End merit special examination and discussion. Although 53.3 percent of the bilingual children thought Italian was a difficult language to understand, speak, read, and write, all thirty children wanted to study Italian formally later on in high school. As they vaguely realized, but could not clearly express, their spoken dialects of southern Italian were somehow different from 'regular' Italian. Their description of 'regular' Italian was understood to mean Standard Italian as opposed to the variety of nonstandard Italian dialects spoken in Avellino, Calabria, and Sicily. Among the bilingual children, 96.7 percent thought they were fortunate to be able to understand and speak Italian. Furthermore, 86.7 percent thought it was a good idea that monolingual children in the North End should study Italian, since the vast majority of the monolinguals' cultural heritage is Italian. When asked if they would want someday to marry someone who could also speak Italian, 53.3 percent responded positively, as did 96.7 percent who wanted their own future children to be able to speak Italian someday. Also, 96.7 percent of the bilinguals thought there are definite advantages in knowing Italian, but at the same time, 96.7 percent also felt that the more English-speaking people they had come to know, the more they wanted to learn to speak English well. Finally, there was not a very strong desire among the bilinguals (only 36.7 percent) to live in Italy.

A number of questions dealt with various aspects of Italian culture: 36.7 percent of the bilinguals responded positively that they regularly listened to and enjoyed Italian music broadcast in the Boston metropolitan area by several Italian-speaking radio stations. All eleven bilinguals (36.7 percent) admitted, however, that their parents were the ones who usually took the initiative to tune in the Italian radio station. Also, 90.0 percent felt comfortable in speaking Italian over the telephone, and only two bilinguals (fourth grade males) knew any jokes in Italian. Moreover, 60.0 percent thought it was a good idea that street signs should also be printed in Italian for the benefit of their parents and friends who might have just arrived from Italy. In their personal religious lives, all thirty bilinguals reported that they spoke English to a priest in the confessional as well as when they recited their prayers or prayed privately to God.

Of the thirty bilinguals, 36.7 percent responded positively that they generally felt more comfortable speaking Italian rather than English because their parents, brothers, and sisters, and older relatives also spoke Italian. However, when asked the question (40) on the language usage questionnaire: 'If you had to choose to speak either Italian or English, what language would you choose, Italian or English?'—66.7 percent of the bilinguals responded that they would choose English because they are now living in the United States, a country where English is the national language. Also, 56.7 percent of the bilinguals thought they were slowly forgetting their Italian, but only 16.7 percent admitted that it would not make a great deal of difference to them personally were they to forget Italian entirely.

Therefore, bilingual children were happy and proud of their ability to understand and speak Italian, of their cultural heritage, and of their ethnic neighborhood. They wished to maintain Italian as a language because they considered it advantageous. However, even though Italian was considered worth knowing and holding on to, nevertheless, bilinguals realized that English is the national language in the United States and it is necessary to know it well for future job opportunities.

Covariation of monolingual children's attitudes toward Italian as a language and toward the North End as an ethnic neighborhood. In addition to knowing how bilingual children think and feel about Italian and their ethnic neighborhood, it is equally important to understand and appreciate how monolinguals look upon Italian as a language and how they esteem their ethnic environment. Only those questions appropriate for monolingual speakers were asked of them in the various questionnaires.

There were fewer monolinguals (20.0 percent) than bilinguals (40.0 percent) who responded positively to the question (1) concerning the possibility of the informant having some best friends who can speak Italian. Although there were more monolinguals (76.7 percent) than bilinguals (53.3 percent) who thought Italian was a difficult language to learn, monolinguals (96.7 percent) considered the ability to understand and speak Italian just as advantageous as did bilinguals (96.7 percent). In fact, monolinguals (93.3 percent) responded positively that they would like to study Italian in high school. Moreover, monolinguals (80.0 percent) thought it was a good idea in general for all non-Italian-Americans to study Italian. Although 36.7 percent of the monolinguals did not want someday to marry an Italian-speaking spouse and only 3.3 percent of them wanted to go to Italy and live there permanently, 53.3 percent of the monolingual children admitted they would prefer their future children to be able someday to speak Italian. As far as intelligence and goodness of Italian-speaking people are concerned, monolinguals thought the Italian-speaking people are smart (56.7

percent) and good (76.7 percent). Only 10.0 percent of the monolinguals thought Italian songs sound better than American songs. Again, when choosing one language over another, Italian or English, 93.3 percent of the monolinguals responded that they would choose English over Italian for the same reasons given by bilinguals: English is the national language spoken in the United States. More important, though, is the fact that a large number of the monolinguals (96.7 percent) felt they should know how to communicate in Italian even though they would prefer knowing English to knowing Italian. They should know Italian precisely because of the large number of Italian-speaking adults and children living and working in the North End of Boston.

Summary

What general conclusions can be drawn from these covariations with respect to the present status of language maintenance and language shift among Italian-American bilingual children living in the North End of Boston? The data clearly point to the presence of an obvious choice of language usage operative on the language behavior of the North End children. There were fundamentally two speech domains which were so divided that as a result, there are at the present time fairly clear norms which guide bilingual children in choosing to communicate in English or in Italian. One of these speech domains is such that communication is carried on 'within the familial environment,' and the other is one in which communication is carried on 'outside the familial environment.' The term 'familial' is used in this discussion to describe a psychological frame of reference within which a bilingual child decides whether or not to choose Italian as the medium of communication for a given speech setting. In general, Italian is spoken by bilingual children when the speech setting is within this familial environment; and English is spoken when the speech setting is outside this familial environment.

Thus, even though there are no geographically isolated language sectors within the North End, and both English and Italian are heard and spoken throughout all parts of this ethnic community, there are well-marked speech settings which guide bilingual children to choose to communicate in either English or Italian.

7
The North End Language Attitudes Study

General Remarks

In the last ten years, there has been a rapidly increasing amount of research in the area of subjective language attitudes. These studies suggest that the evaluation which a listener is likely to give to a person's speech will generally depend heavily upon his previously formed attitudes toward the particular dialect, ethnic membership, and socioeconomic class of that speaker. By the word 'attitude' is meant the inclination to react in a particular manner in response to certain situations or variances of behavior. The phenomenon of listening, evaluating, and then judging a speaker on the basis of his speech is quite common, especially when two people are first introduced to each other. In this initial period of communication with one another, each interlocutor, while listening to the other person speak, generally assigns not only a tentative geographical locus where the speaker may have been born, raised, and educated, but he might also try to determine his ethnic identification and socioeconomic status. Even in situations in which listeners are not able to depend on visual cues of speakers, such as when listening to someone speak on the telephone or from a tape recording, they can often identify with considerable consistency the sex, socioeconomic status, and ethnicity of the speaker. In fact, it has been found that language reveals much information about a speaker's status even to nonlinguistically trained listeners such as grade school children (Harms 1961, 1963; Shuy, Baratz, and Wolfram 1970; Shuy and Fasold 1971).

Although there are a number of linguists who are keenly interested in determining the constants which affect a listener in identifying a speaker according to his age, sex, educational level, socioeconomic status, and ethnicity, not very much is yet known about what specific linguistic and extralinguistic cues affect the listener's evaluation and subsequent judgment of the speaker. Although it is not our purpose here to exhaustively enumerate the results of research in subjective language attitudes, it is important to note that much research into subjective reaction has reveleted trends or patterns which seem quite similar to those yielded by objective linguistic data.

Lambert and his associates (Lambert 1960; Anisfeld and Lambert 1964) indicate that subjective evaluations of speech are systematically affected by associations made with stereotype categories held about a variety of majority and minority groups. Williams (1973) reported similar findings in his research. He maintains the thesis that persons tend to employ stereotyped sets of attitudes as 'anchor points' for their evaluation of whatever is presented to them as a sample of a person's speech.

Labov's (1966) extensive study of the social stratification of speech in New York City resulted in drawing attention to the importance of the relationship between speech and social class. Speakers from different social levels are characterized by distributive phonological, lexical, and syntactic features which are easily identified by linguistically naive judges and which may be used by these judges as a basis for evaluating the speakers. Ellis (1967) also showed that naive judges speaking one particular regional dialect of American English can accurately identify the social status of persons speaking different dialects. Markel, Eisler, and Reese (1967) have also shown that in the United States, regional dialects are a significant factor in judging personality from speech style.

It has been pointed out by many linguists (Shuy, Baratz, and Wolfram 1970:1) that Labov's pioneering efforts provided a useful empirical model for a number of similar research projects. Working with five phonological features, Labov found that the subjective reactions of his informants were inarticulate and below the level of conscious self-awareness (Labov 1967:405). He also discovered that there is no specific vocabulary of socially meaningful terms with which his informants were able to evaluate speech. Although New Yorkers typically held strong views about the speech of their city, there were only a few informants who could cite specific words or phrases which adequately characterized what they meant. One of the many advances made in linguistics which was directly related to Labov's exploratory work is in the area of field methodology. Labov substantiated his field procedures with well-documented evidence that tape-recorded natural utterances of speakers are superior to synthetic representations made by experimenters.

There is an additional aspect of the relationship between language and social class which Labov's (1967) study of social mobility has well exemplified. Upwardly mobile people tend to adopt the linguistic style of the socioeconomic group just above their own. Brown (1969) reported similar findings in his French Canadian study. He found that speech styles of different socioeconomic levels can be accurately described by listeners, mainly on the basis of a dichotomy between upper class and lower class. Brown suggests that French Canadians tend to model their speech on those with whom they identify; for example, those who are upwardly mobile will tend to adopt upper class speech features.

There have also been a number of empirical studies carried out in several countries which suggest that regional variable dialects might elicit conditioned value judgments which in turn affect the attitudes of listeners toward speakers from various cultural and linguistic backgrounds. For example, a speaker may be judged favorably or unfavorably by the prestige of the particular dialect the speaker uses. Giles (1970) reported similar findings in English, while Tucker (1968) reported that speakers of American English were viewed more favorably by listeners in the Philippines than were speakers of Filipino English or of Tagalog.

Lambert (1967) discovered some interesting data in his bilingual research with French and English Canadian university students. They were asked to rate the personality characteristics of ten speakers—five English and five French. The experiment was set up so that in reality five bilingual speakers were used, with each speaker appearing in two guises. English students evaluated the English-speaking guises much more favorably on most traits, while French students not only evaluated English guises more favorably that French guises, but also evaluated the French guises significantly less favorably than did the English students.

Finally, Shuy, Baratz, and Wolfram (1970) described the results of a statistical analysis of subjective judgment data involving Detroit's respondents' evaluations of five types of English speech: Detroit speech, White Southern speech, British speech, Black speech, and Standard speech. There were a number of interesting results from this study, one of which indicated that black listeners did only slightly better than whites in identifying black speakers, and whites did only slightly better than blacks in judging white speakers. Also, age did not particularly increase the listeners' ability to determine the race of a speaker: children, teenagers, and adults varied only 2.4 percent in their ability to identify black speakers. Shuy, Baratz, and Wolfram's study of subjective language attitudes clearly inspired and guided the present North End language attitudes study. The North End study not only modeled on their fieldwork methodology, but it also followed their clear delineation of procedural criteria of extracting, analyzing, and synthesizing the language attitudes data.

Purpose and Rationale

The purpose of the North End Language Attitudes Study was threefold: first, to investigate and measure the North End children's ability to discern extralinguistic factors such as age, educational grade level, sex, race, and ethnicity in a variety of speakers; second, to discern and assess the role such factors have in accurately identifying the speakers; third, to assess the attitudes of the North End children toward a number of socioethnic speech samples.

Throughout the United States there is a wide range of social, ethnic, and regional variation in the manner in which Americans speak English. These variations range from phonological differences (e.g., [kriːk] vs. [krIk] for *creek*) and lexical (e.g. *soda* vs. *pop*) to syntactic ones (e.g. *He ain't got nobody* vs. *He doesn't have anyone*). These phonological, lexical, and syntactic variations have been shown to be not random but distributed in systematic patterns within various speech communities of American English. In fact, recent investigators of language behavior of whites, blacks, and Puerto Ricans have shown that there are definite linguistic features which correlate with extralinguistic factors such as age, sex, socioeconomic status, and ethnicity (Shuy 1967; Stewart 1967, 1968; Fasold 1972; Wolfram 1969, 1974). Studies by Rey (1974) and Rosenthal (1974) have also shown that attitudes of listeners such as employers and grade school children strongly affect their relationship with a vareity of speakers.

There were a number of research questions which were raised with respect to the North End children's reactions toward a number of speech samples. These questions were used to establish a clear working methodology in finding, analyzing, and synthesizing the language attitudes data. The eight research questions are:

(1) How accurately can North End children correctly identify the age, grade, sex, ethnicity, and so on of a speaker only from a sample of his spoken language?
(2) How important is age of the North End children in correctly identifying speakers?
(3) Do male and female North End children perform equally well in identifying the social variables of a speaker?
(4) Does accurate identification of a speaker increase if a North End child himself possesses attributes similar to those of the speaker (i.e. can a bilingual Italian-American child identify more with another bilingual Italian-American than with a monolingual Italian-American?)
(5) Can North End children make reliable judgments on a binary semantic differential in response to speech samples?
(6) Is there a difference in responses to white speech and black speech on the binary semantic differential by North End children?
(7) Do various responses on the binary semantic differential to various types of speech vary with age, sex, and ethnicity of the speaker?
(8) Do monolinguals and bilinguals respond differently to the language concepts presented in this study?

Methodology

The basic instrument used in this attitudes study was a tape recording of speech samples of twelve informants representing different age, sex, and ethnicity factors. The selection of informants was limited to black and white male and female children between the ages of six and fourteen from three cities: Boston's North End, Detroit, and Washington, D.C. In selecting the informants by random sampling, the following criteria were used: (1) the informant should be a resident of a city for at least five years; and (2) the informant's speech should be evaluated by at least three linguists as representative in terms of particular linguistic features of the age, sex, and ethnic group to which the speaker was assigned.

The speech passages chosen for the North End study were taken from three sources: (1) informal conversational sections of the North End interview tapes; (2) informal conversational sections of the Detroit Dialect Study interview tapes; and (3) informal conversational speech samples of children of Washington, D.C. interview tapes. Shuy, Baratz, and Wolfram indicate (1970) that although this particular method of test construction departs from traditional methods in which different speakers representing various social variables read identical passages, they believe that there are sound linguistic reasons for selecting spontaneous speech samples. 'In the first place, it gives a degree of naturalness not found in the traditional technique. Furthermore, the variety of topics makes the task more interesting. Finally, this method allows for certain grammatical alternants which would not be realized if speakers from different classes were simply reading the same passage' (1970:6). The North End Language Attitudes test followed, then, Shuy, Baratz, and Wolfram's suggestion to use informal or spontaneous speech samples according to the following two criteria: (1) the linguistic features representing the age, sex, and ethnicity of the speaker should be found in the passage (e.g. despirantized interdental fricatives such as *those three boys over in that boat* in the speech of the North End children); and (2) the passage should be culturally unmarked (e.g. no reference to socially or ethnically characteristic behavior such as the St. Anthony summer festival familiar to all North End children). Since the assumption was that the 148 respondents in the study were to react only on the basis of the linguistic variables, the evaluation of the twelve speech samples as 'representative' of the informants' social and ethnic group was based on a comparison of the linguistic variables made by a team of one professional linguist and two doctoral candidates in linguistics. They ultimately were responsible for judging the informants' speech as typical of the particular social and ethnic group they were chosen to represent.

Selected passages for each of the twelve tape recorded speech samples were excerpted from the spontaneous conversational sections of the interviews in which the plots of movies and television programs were discussed by the informants. These narrative sections yielded the most useful passages in terms of comparable cultural content. Each of the twelve passages was seventy seconds in length. With the exception of one passage, none of the twelve passages needed any editing. In this one passage, editing was done in order to eliminate several words describing the cultural content of the passage. The end result of selecting the appropriate passages was twelve recorded passages dealing with movie or television narratives which were relatively comparable in their cultural content. The completed tape, then, included twelve speech samples, each of which was seventy seconds in length, and each passage was repeated twice. The length of the entire tape was twenty-six minutes and forty-three seconds. Table 7.1 indicates the twelve speakers and their respective age, grade, sex, ethnicity, race, place of birth, and the city in which they are currently living.

7 The North End language-attitudes study / 117

Table 7.1. Psycholinguistic attitude tape recording with speech samples of twelve informants according to age, grade, sex, race, ethnicity, place of birth, and present residence

Sample Number	Age	Grade	Sex	Race	Ethnicity	Place of birth	Present residence
1	14	8	M	W	Italian-American monolingual	Boston	North End
2	9	4	F	B	American monolingual	Detroit	Detroit
3	10	5	F	B	American monolingual	Detroit	Detroit
4	14	8	M	W	American monolingual	Wash.D.C.	Washington
5	11	4	F	W	Italian-American bilingual	Naples	North End
6	10	4	F	W	Italian-American monolingual	Boston	North End
7	14	8	M	B	American monolingual	Wash.D.C.	Washington
8	14	8	M	W	Italian-American bilingual	Palermo	North End
9	11	6	M	B	American monolingual	Detroit	Detroit
10	9	4	M	W	Italian-American monolingual	Boston	North End
11	10	4	F	W	American monolingual	Detroit	Detroit
12	9	4	F	W	Italian-American monolingual	Boston	North End

The pilot study. Before the Language Attitudes Study tape was used on the 148 students, several pre-testing experiments with the tape were conducted with the aid of ten second and ten fifth grade male and female North End children. The purpose of the pilot testing was to determine: (1) if the instructions were adequate and if the test could indeed be completed within an hour's time; (2) if the acoustic quality of the tape was adequate for use in the high ceilinged, relatively large classrooms which are typical of old schools such as the ones in the North End; and (3) if the different age and class levels could adequately handle the task which was being requested of them.

The pilot testing indicated that the Language Attitudes test could be completed within one's hour allotted time. No student in the pilot testing indicated any difficulty in adequately hearing the tape even in the large classrooms. Finally, although the instructions describing the task of the test were understood, some minor revisions were made based on suggestions by the students who participated in the pre-testing and by the teachers present during the pre-testing. More important, however, is the fact that when the second graders found the task of the Language Attitudes pre-test too complex, it was decided to administer the test to only one class of first graders during the actual testing period. This procedure was adopted in order to see whether or not first grade children were actually capable of achieving the task of the test. If the first graders were found to be capable, then the same test would have been given to the other two classes of first graders. However, when the test was given to the one class of first graders with guarded expectations, the results of the test definitely confirmed the suspicion that the test's task was too confusing for the vast majority of first graders. Therefore, the fourth and eighth graders in all three schools were the only informants to be tested subsequently.

Instructions. The actual testing was done only by the author. No teachers were present during the hour's testing period. The standard instructions were as follows:

> Instructions. I'd be very grateful to all of you if you would help me find out a few things about how some people talk. I'd like to see how much you can tell me about a person just from the way he talks. You know you can tell a lot about someone just from hearing him on the telephone. Well, this is about the same kind of information I'm interested in getting.
>
> In a little while, I'm going to ask you to listen to twelve different speakers on this tape recorder. These speakers are talking about different movies and television programs they have enjoyed seeing. Some of the speakers on the tape are black and some are white; some of them are from the North End and some are not; some were born in Italy and some were not.
>
> First, I'd like to see if you can identify each of the twelve speakers according to the questions numbered one through six. Second, I'd like to see how you think the speaker on the tape sounds

to you according to questions numbered seven through twenty-one. There may be some cases that you are not sure, but just try to make the best guess you can. For each question, circle only *one* of the two underlined words, but in questions two and six, write your answers on the line. Please don't write any of your answers until I've finished playing each speaker's voice a second time. You'll have plenty of time to write your answers after I play the speaker's voice a second time. O.K.?

Now let's read together each of the twenty-one questions to make sure we all understand what the underlined words mean. [Clarifying answers to the children's questions regarding either the task's instructions or the meaning of any words were then given.] O.K.? Let's begin. [Play tape]

The time allotted for the respondents to write their appropriate answers to all twenty-one items was ninety seconds. The entire North End Language Attitudes test took fifty minutes to complete.

Questionnaire. The Language Attitudes Study questionnaire was divided into two sections. Section one was concerned with responses regarding the speaker's age, grade, sex, race, place of birth, and finally, whether or not the speaker was from the North End neighborhood. Section two consisted of a response sheet for the binary semantic differential of language concepts. For each of the twelve sample speech passages, all 148 respondents were asked to listen carefully to each of the tape recorded speakers. After listening to the second repetition of each of the twelve passages, the respondents were asked to judge the speaker according to the twenty-one items. The format for each of the twelve stimuli is as follows.

LANGUAGE ATTITUDES TEST
1. Is this speaker a *boy* or a *girl*? (Circle your answer)
2. What grade in school is this speaker? _____
3. Is this speaker *black* or *white*?
4. Is this speaker from our North End area? Yes – No
5. Does he/she sound as if he/she was born in Italy? Yes – No
6. How old do you think this speaker is? _____

This speaker:
7. has a *bad* or *nice* voice.
8. speaks *fast* or *slow*.
9. is a *good* or *bad* person.
10. sounds *dumb* or *smart*.
11. sounds *happy* or *sad*.
12. sounds *ugly* or *nice*.
13. sounds *calm* or *scared*.
14. sounds *friendly* or *unfriendly*.
15. is *older* or *younger* than you.
16. speaks *with* or *without* an Italian accent.
17. sounds *lazy* or *energetic*.

18. sounds *comfortable* or *uncomfortable*.
19. sounds like a *cold* or *warm* person.
20. is *easy* or *hard* to understand.
21. sounds *honest* or *dishonest*.

Results

The data in this study are based upon the responses of 148 students, of whom seventy-seven (or 52.0 percent) were fourth graders and seventy-one (or 48.0 percent) were eighth graders. All 148 respondents were white; sixty-nine (or 46.6 percent) were males and seventy-nine (or 53.4 percent) were females. There were eighty-five (or 57.4 percent) monolingual speakers and sixty-three (or 42.6 percent) bilinguals. All 148 respondents lived in the North End and attended one of the three parochial schools in the area.

Table 7.2. The North End 148 respondents according to grade-age, sex, and ethnicity

	Fourth grade		Eighth grade	
	Males	Females	Males	Females
Monolinguals	23	18	19	25
Bilinguals	14	22	13	14
	37	40	32	39

Total sample = 148

Grade-age identification. 1. *Can North End children correctly identify the grade-age of a person from a sample of his spoken language?* The results of the Language Attitudes test indicated that, on the whole, the North End respondents correctly identified the grade-age of all twelve speakers 59.2 percent of the time. It is interesting to note, however, that not only did more respondents correctly identify the grade-ages of black speakers (87.5 percent) than white speakers (50.0 percent), but they also correctly identified more North End residents (62.1 percent).

1a. *What is the effect of the age of the listener on his ability to identify correctly the age of a speaker?* There were more fourth graders (77.1 percent) than eighth graders (47.1 percent) who correctly identified the ages of the twelve speakers. With respect to race, more fourth graders (82.3 percent) than eighth graders (41.0 percent) indicated correctly the ages of black speakers. Also, fourth graders were found to be more correct in identifying North Enders (78.1 percent) than eighth graders (49.3 percent).

1b. *What is the effect of the sex of the listener on his ability to identify correctly the age of a speaker?* Female listeners correctly identified the ages of the twelve speakers 64.7 percent of the time and males did so 53.4 percent.

1c. *What is the effect of the ethnicity of the listener on his ability to identify correctly the age of a speaker?* It was found that more monolingual speakers

(68.2 percent) than bilingual speakers (51.0 percent) were able to identify correctly the ages of the twelve speakers. Table 7.3 shows the effect of grade-age, sex, and ethnicity of all 148 North End respondents in their correct identification of the five social variables of all twelve speakers.

Table 7.3. Effect of grade-age, sex, and ethnicity of all 148 listeners upon the identification of grade-age, sex, ethnicity, race, and residency of the twelve speakers

Respondents	Age	Sex	Ethnicity	Race	Residency
All 148	59.2	71.1	80.5	77.2	61.1
Grade					
4	77.1	70.7	76.6	72.3	52.5
8	47.1	73.0	84.9	82.0	68.1
Sex					
Males	53.4	68.2	82.7	76.5	64.4
Females	64.7	70.7	85.0	77.0	66.3
Ethnicity					
Monolinguals	68.2	74.1	85.3	81.6	69.3
Bilinguals	51.0	69.7	74.7	70.4	54.2

Sex Identification. 2. Can North End children correctly identify the sex of a person from a sample of his spoken language? It was found that the 148 respondents correctly identified the sex of the twelve speakers 71.1 percent of the time. The respondents were also more correct in identifiying the sex of white speakers (78.3 percent) than black speakers (56.8 percent); they were also more correct in identifiying the sex of North End residents (88.3 percent) than non-North End residents (72.8 percent).

2a. What is the effect of the grade-age of the listener on his ability to identify correctly the sex of a speaker? Eighth graders identified the sexual identity of the twelve speakers slightly better (73.0 percent) than fourth graders (70.7 percent). However, the fourth graders recognized more female speakers as female 52.4 percent of the time and eighth graders did so 53.5 percent; fourth graders recognized male speakers as male 89.0 percent of the time and eighth graders did so 92.5 percent. Therefore, more male speakers were recognized as males than female speakers as female.

2b. What is the effect of the sex of the listener on his ability to identify correctly the sex of a speaker? For all practical purposes, there was no significant difference between male respondents and female respondents because male respondents correctly identified the sex of speakers 68.2 percent of the time while females did so 70.7 percent.

2c. *What is the effect of the ethnicity of the listener on his ability to identify correctly the sex of a speaker?* More monolinguals (85.3 percent) than bilinguals (62.9 percent) correctly identified the sex of speakers. Table 7.3 indicates the percentages of correct identifications of the twelve speakers' sexual identity according to the listeners' grade-age, sex and ethnicity.

Ethnicity identification. 3. *Can North End children correctly identify the ethnicity of a person from a sample of his spoken language?* The respondents correctly identified the ethnicity of the speakers 80.5 percent of time; that is, if any of the twelve speakers sounded as if he or she were born in Italy, as Speakers 5 and 8, then that speaker was necessarily judged as bilingual. Although not every bilingual child in the North End was born in Italy, all bilingual children spoke English with some Italian phonological influence ranging on a continuum from a heavy accent to one that was marked by only an occasional but noticeable Italian phonological carryover. Although ethnicity of the speakers was correctly identified 80.5 percent, the respondents tended to identify more American born speakers (88.9 percent) than Italian born ones (38.2 percent).

3a. *What is the effect of the grade-age of the listener on his ability to identify correctly the ethnicity of a speaker?* The fourth graders correctly identified the ethnicity of the twelve speakers 76.6 percent of the time, while eighth graders did so 84.9 percent. While eighth graders were better in correctly identifying monolinguals (92.7 percent) than fourth graders (80.7 percent), for all practical purposes, both eighth graders (45.8 percent) and fourth graders (45.3 percent) had identical scores for identifying bilinguals.

3b. *What is the effect of the sex of the listener on his ability to identify correctly the ethnicity of a speaker?* The respondents' answers indicated that slightly more females (85.0 percent) than males (82.7 percent) were correct in identifying the ethnicity of the speakers.

3c. *What is the effect of the ethnicity of the listener on his ability to identify correctly the ethnicity of a speaker?* In general, more tape-recorded monolingual speakers were correctly identified as monolinguals (85.3 percent) than bilingual speakers as bilinguals (74.7 percent). Specifically, monolingual respondents correctly identified more monolingual speakers (89.5 percent) than bilingual speakers (10.6 percent); also bilinguals identified more monolingual speakers (73.0 percent) than bilingual speakers (31.7 percent). Table 7.3 shows the percentages of correct identification of the twelve speakers' ethnicity according to the listeners' grade-age, sex, and ethnicity.

Race identification. 4. *Can North End children correctly identify the race of a person from a sample of his spoken language?* The responses made by all 148 North End children indicated that they correctly identified the race of each of the twelve speakers 77.2 percent of the time. They identified slightly more white speakers (77.2 percent) than black speakers (74.2 percent). Of the white speakers, the respondents were able to identify correctly only slightly more non-North End residents (79.4 percent) than North End residents (76.5 percent).

4a. What is the effect of the grade-age of the listener on his ability to identify correctly the race of a speaker? In general, fourth graders correctly identified the race of the speakers less often (72.3 percent) than eighth graders (82.0 percent). Fourth graders identified black speakers as black 68.5 percent of the time and white speakers as white 68.8 percent. Eighth graders identified black speakers as black 80.2 percent of the time and white speakers as white 82.9 percent. There does not appear, therefore, to be any significant advantage of grade-age with respect to identifying correctly the race of a speaker since both fourth and eighth grade children had only slightly different percentages in identifying black speakers as black and white speakers as white: 68.5 vs. 68.8 percents for fourth graders and 80.2 vs. 82.9 percents for eighth graders.

4b. What is the effect of the sex of the listener on his ability to identify correctly the race of a speaker? For all practical purposes, females correctly identified the race of the twelve speakers (77.0 percent) just as well as males (76.5 percent). Females identified black speakers as black 78.5 percent of the time while they identified white speakers as white 76.2 percent. Males indicated comparable results for they identified black speakers as black 80.6 percent and white speakers as white 74.5 percent. The data indicate, therefore, that sex does not appear to contribute significantly to the identification of race.

4c. What is the effect of the ethnicity of the listener on his ability to identify correctly the race of a speaker? Monolingual listeners identified white speakers as white 90.6 percent of the time and black speakers as black 45.6 percent. Bilingual speakers, however, correctly identified white speakers as white 81.0 percent and black speakers as black 46.3 percent. Table 7.3 shows the percentages of correct identification of the twelve speakers' race according to the listeners' grade-age, sex, and ethnicity.

Residency identification. 5. Can North End children correctly identify whether or not a speaker currently lives in the North End from a sample of his spoken language? North End children correctly identified the proper place of residence 61.1 percent of the time. The 148 respondents were correct more often in identifying non-North End residents (64.5 percent) than North End residents (53.8 percent).

5a. What is the effect of the grade-age of the listener on his ability to identify correctly the current residence of a speaker? Fourth graders were less correct (52.5 percent) than eighth graders (68.1 percent) in identifying the residency of the twelve speakers. Also, fourth graders correctly judged more non-North End residents (59.3 percent) than North End residents (45.7 percent) as did the eighth graders: 78.4 percent for non-North End residents and 57.7 percent for North End residents.

5b. What is the effect of sex of the listener on his ability to identify correctly the current residence of a speaker? In general, there were slightly more females (66.3) than males (64.3 percent) who correctly determined whether or not the speakers were from the North End. Furthermore, both males and females had lower percentages for correctly identifying North End residents (females: 57.8 percent and males: 53.4 percent) than for non-North End residents (females: 74.7 percent and males: 75.3 percent).

5c. What is the effect of the ethnicity of the listener on his ability to identify correctly the current residence of a speaker? Monolingual listeners correctly identified the proper residency for speakers 69.3 percent and bilinguals did so 54.2 percent. More monolinguals (55.1 percent) than bilinguals (43.7 percent) were able to correctly determine North End residents. Table 7.3 indicates the percentages of correct identification of the twelve speakers' place of residency according to the listeners' grade-age, sex, and ethnicity.

In comparing the responses made by the 148 informants of the Language Attitudes test as shown in Table 7.3, a well-ordered pattern emerges. First, with respect to the grade-age of the respondents, eighth graders were more correct than fourth graders in identifying the sex, ethnicity, race, and residency of the twelve speakers, except in the case of the *grade-age* variable of the twelve speakers. There does not seem to be any significant reason to explain this anomaly other than the fact that of the twelve speakers, seven speakers were either in the fourth or fifth grades, while four speakers were either in the eighth or ninth grades and the remaining speaker was in the sixth grade. Thus, there is a slight possibility that the fourth grade respondents were somehow affected by the majority of the speakers who were clustered around the fourth grade.

The second pattern emerging from Table 7.3 shows that in every instance of identifying the five social variables of the speakers, more female than male respondents were found to be more correct in identifying the given social variables. The third pattern which emerges shows that more monolinguals than bilinguals were correct in identifying all five social variables of the twelve speakers.

Binary semantic differential judgments. For the binary semantic differential analysis, it was decided to investigate the answers of the 148 respondents in terms of the twelve speakers' dialects. As a result, all twelve speakers' speech samples were studied and were then categorized as either (1) Standard American English; (2) Nonstandard Italian-American English; or (3) Nonstandard Black English. Thus, Speakers 4 and 11 were judged to be representative of Standard American English; Speakers 1, 5, 6, 8, 10, and 12 of Nonstandard Italian-American English; and Speakers 2, 3, 7, and 9 of Nonstandard Black English.

The fifteen binary semantic differential items, numbered seven through twenty-one on the Language Attitudes test, were divided into five categories. Number 15 was omitted from this classification because number 15 was related to grade-age and, consequently, tabulated with the grade-age identification discussed below. Each of the remaining fourteen items were placed in one of the five categories which characterized the speakers in terms of their (1) intelligence, (2) emotions, (3) disposition, (4) virtues, and (5) voice quality. The descriptive word-pairs for each of the speech concepts are listed in one of the five categories below.

(1) **Intelligence** 10. dumb-smart
(2) **Emotions** 11. happy-sad
  13. calm-scared
  18. comfortable-uncomfortable
  19. cold-warm
(3) **Disposition** 12. ugly-nice
  14. friendly-unfriendly
  17. lazy-energetic
(4) **Virtues** 9. good-bad
  21. honest-dishonest
(5) **Voice quality** 7. bad-nice
  8. fast-slow
  16. with-without Italian accent
  20. easy-hard to understand

Table 7.4 shows the percentages of responses made by all 148 North End respondents. Note that the percentages reflect the responses made for the positive items of the descriptive word-pairs such as (11) *happy* as in *happy* or *sad*; (10) *smart* as in *dumb* or *smart*; (17) *energetic* as in *lazy* or *energetic*.

Table 7.4. Responses of 148 North End children to binary semantic differential speech concepts according to the categories of intelligence, emotions, disposition, virtues, and voice quality

Intelligence	Standard American English	Nonstandard Ital-American English	Nonstandard Black English
10. smart	82.4	65.0	47.5
Emotions			
11. happy	77.3	71.4	57.6
13. calm	71.6	52.9	50.8
18. comfortable	68.9	56.9	46.8
19. warm	68.9	62.5	47.6
Disposition			
12. nice	82.4	65.4	49.3
14. friendly*	78.4	80.6	60.4
17. energetic	79.1	64.2	42.1

Table 7.4 Continued

	Standard American English	Nonstandard Ital-American English	Nonstandard Black English
Virtues			
9. good	91.1	80.8	62.1
21. honest	87.3	80.0	65.2
Voice quality			
7. nice	82.4	65.4	49.3
8. slow*	35.5	43.6	58.8
16. with accent*	12.8	38.1	16.3
20. easy	59.5	38.1	24.5

With the exception of items 8, 14, and 16 in the Language Attitudes test (marked with an asterisk), Standard American English was the dialect which consistently had the highest frequencies of favorable attitudes; Nonstandard Black English had the lowest favorable frequencies; and Nonstandard Italian-American English had intermediate frequencies. Note that item 8 (speaks *fast* or *slow*) is actually a neutral speech concept, since speaking either fast or slow is, linguistically speaking, indifferent. What makes speaking fast or slow favorable or unfavorable is the clear articulation and comprehensibility with which the speaker's message is communicated to a listener. However, many more black speakers were judged as having the slowest speech delivery style (58.8 percent) of all three groups of speakers. Furthermore, item 14 (sounds *friendly* or *unfriendly*) was the only item which the North End respondents judged the most favorable quality of those who spoke Nonstandard Italian-American English. Finally, item 16 (speaks *with* or *without* an Italian accent) was analyzed in terms of which group of speakers was judged to speak with an Italian accent. Speakers of Nonstandard Italian-American English were judged to have the highest frequency, 38.1 percent.

In conclusion, the hierarchically ordered percentages for all three dialects in relationship to the positive speech concept for each of the eleven binary items indicate that a general pattern favoring Standard American English is present. The responses by the 148 respondents reflected stronger positive feelings and more favorable attitudes toward speakers whose speech is marked by Standard American English linguistic features than toward either their own Nonstandard Italian-American English (second most favored) or those who speak Nonstandard Black English (least favored). Finally, when the binary semantic differential speech concepts were further analyzed in terms of the effect of grade-age, sex, and ethnicity of the 148 respondents, no significant patterns emerged; there was no difference between responses made by fourth and eighth graders or between males and females or between monolinguals and bilinguals.

Summary

In conclusion, then, from the summarized data displayed in Table 7.3, it seems relatively clear that the 148 North End respondents of both grades, sexes, and ethnicities performed fairly well in identifying the five social variables of the twelve speakers. With the exception of the anomaly found in the speakers' grade-age category among the fourth grade respondents, there is a well-ordered hierarchical pattern found not only among the respondents in a number of ways (e.g. eighth graders had higher percentages in correct identifications than fourth graders), but most especially among the five social variables of the speakers. The general hierarchically arranged pattern discovered for the speakers' variables ranging from higher to lower percentages of correct identifications is first, ethnicity, then race, sex, residency, and finally, grade-age. The only exception found to contradict this hierarchical pattern was the anomaly of the fourth graders' responses to the speakers' grade-age variable. The hierarchically ranked pattern of the speakers' social variable was one of the most significant results of our research into the ability of a listener to identify correctly the various social variables in a number of speech samples. The data indicated that the 148 respondents have a tendency to be more accurate in identifying a speaker's ethnicity, race, and sex than his residency or grade-age.

It is also interesting to note that not only did the eighth grade respondents do better in general than fourth graders in identifying the speakers' social variables, but females also did better than male respondents in correctly identifying the same five variables. Furthermore, monolingual listeners indicated by their higher percentages that they have more of an ability than bilinguals in correctly identifying the ethnicity, race, sex, residency, and grade-age of a variety of speakers.

On the basis of the data displayed in Table 7.4 for the binary semantic differential in response to speech samples and language concepts, it is clear that although the North End respondents may be unable to articulate why they might consider Standard American English as sounding any better than their own dialect or the dialects of Black English speakers, nevertheless the responses to the binary semantic differential scale resulted in the three hierarchically stratified dialects. It appears, therefore, that the binary semantic differential responses to speech samples suggest that value judgments were being placed on those linguistic features which are used to identify social variables such as ethnicity, race, sex, and so on. The respondents' answers to each of the fourteen binary descriptive word-pairs tend to confirm data culled from participant observation that the majority of North End children are racially prejudiced; Nonstandard Black English had the lowest percentages for all fourteen positive descriptive speech concepts.

8
Summary and Conclusions

This study has been concerned with investigating the linguistic development and socialization process of monolingual and bilingual Italian-American children living in Boston's North End. We have dealt particularly with the differences found in three linguistic variables in nonstandard Italian-American English. Correlations between these three linguistic features and social factors were made to determine the influence of extralinguistic factors on the speech of monolingual and bilingual children in this predominantly Italian ethnic community. Stylistic variations of the Italian-American children's language behavior were also studied and found in general to be systematized. Administered tests indicated clearly defined sociolinguistic patterning of the social variables of grade-age, sex, and ethnicity with the three linguistic variables under investigation. Furthermore, when both the nature and degree of maintaining Italian or shifting from Italian to English were studied, it was found that well-marked social contexts provide bilingual Italian-American children with general guidelines for choosing either Italian or English. Finally, a large number of Italian-American children's subjective reactions to a variety of American English speech samples were tested and analyzed for any significant patterns.

There has been a void in the literature of a systematic analysis of the particular aspects encompassing language and cultural differences among monolingual and bilingual children living in various Italian-American communities in the United States. Child language acquisition literature, on the other hand, has provided a general developmental framework for the acquisition of language in children as well as a model for research into the acquisition of communicative competence. However, this body of literature has generally concerned itself with competence and performance related to actual language use, rather than investigating the development of social awareness of language acculturation of any specific ethnic group. This study, modeled principally on Labov's (1966), Wolfram's (1969, 1974), and Fasold's (1972) methodologies, represents one attempt to help fill such voids in the literature by providing a general research model for investigating the language socialization of various Italian ethnic communities scattered throughout the United States.

8 Summary and conclusions

The Three Research Questions

We have attempted to delineate specifically and systematically the ongoing, dynamic linguistic and cultural aspects influencing the language behavior of the Italian-American children of the North End. In Chapter 1 we posed three questions to which the study would be addressed. We are now in a position to provide answers to each of them.

1. How are Italian and/or English used by monolingual and bilingual children in the North End?

There were fundamentally two speech domains which were so divided that, as a result, we can now point out fairly clear norms which guide bilingual children in choosing to communicate in English or Italian. In one of these two speech domains, communication is carried on 'within the familial environment,' and in the other, communication is carried on 'outside the familial environment.'

It must be recalled that the respondents were asked to state what language(s) they spoke *now* and *with whom*. Italian was found to be the stronger of the two languages within the familial environment. Bilingual children reflected in their answers to the various questionnaires not only a psychologically wholesome and accepting common sense attitude, but also a very reasonable and mature outlook toward speaking Italian. Thus, they spoke Italian without any embarrassment with their parents inside or outside the home, in the North End neighborhood, or in the downtown area. In a wider social context, bilingual children also felt this independence and maturity toward Italian when speaking with grandparents, aunts, and uncles. Even shopkeepers were considered within the familial environment, presumably because they were trustworthy adults who did not pose a threat to the bilinguals' sense of security by making embarrassing remarks. Bilingual children also spoke Italian with their brothers and sisters at home alone. If monolingual children were to come to the bilingual's home to play, then a bilingual child would speak English with his siblings in the presence of the monolinguals.

There was a shift from Italian to English when a bilingual child moved into an area outside the familial environment, into an area in which he no longer felt secure, when he no longer felt that he was being accepted for what *he is as a person*, but for what *his linguistic background has been*. Thus, bilingual children shifted from Italian to English when monolingual children mixed in a group of bilingual children on the school playground at recess time or on the street after school.

Parents have a very strong cultural influence on the linguistic development of their bilingual children. The majority of these children's immigrant parents are not anxious to perfect their own ability to communicate in English. They usually wish only to be able to communicate enough in English to get along in stores and shops outside the North End. However, they have very high socioeconomic and educational goals for their children. Consequently, immigrant parents are not at all personally resentful that their children speak

English; they understand that for their children's own benefit, their children must be capable of understanding, speaking, reading, and writing English very well, in order to excel in all of their school subjects. Nevertheless, even with these values and goals of education, the majority of immigrant parents not only desire but demand quite vigorously that Italian continue to be spoken within the home in the parent-child and sibling-sibling relationships.

Thus, even though there are no geographically isolated language sectors within the North End, and both English and Italian are spoken throughout all parts of the North End, there are well-marked speech settings which guide bilingual children to choose to communicate in either English or Italian.

2. What are the linguistic differences between American English speech of monolingual children and bilingual children with respect to various social factors such as grade-age, sex, and ethnicity?

The data for the variable analysis of interdental fricatives, word-final consonant cluster simplification, and third person singular present tense verb concord yielded variable rules for the widely recognized and socially stigmatized linguistic features of despirantization, cluster simplification, and Z_3 deletion. Each of these variable rules indicated a number of hierarchically ordered constraints which manifested in varying degrees their influence in promoting despirantization, cluster simplification, or Z_3 deletion in the speech of Italian-American children.

When the three linguistic variables under investigation were correlated with the social factor of grade-age, it was discovered that a consistent pattern appeared: fourth graders had the highest frequencies of usage of all three socially stigmatized linguistic features; the eighth graders the lowest; first graders had intermediate frequency rates.

It is interesting to note that Rosenthal (1974) demonstrated in her study of the acquisition of children's awareness of language differences that preschool children as young as three years old are able to discriminate, categorize, and express specific attitudes toward Standard American English and Black English. Rosenthal discovered that, although the development of social awareness of language differences may begin as early as age three, the largest increase in the development of such awareness occurs between the ages of four and five.

The results of the North End data, however, were contrary to the expected developmental linguistic behavior of North End children normally acquiring their native language or a second language (i.e. English). In general, compared to fourth and eighth graders, first graders would be expected to make more 'mistakes' while learning a language and to be inconsistent in distinguishing between socially stigmatized forms and prestigious ones. First graders would also be expected to be less aware than fourth graders of the social aspects of implications in using socially stigmatized forms in their speech. In other words, fourth graders would be expected to use less stigmatized forms than first graders, since the former group has gained through social maturity more linguistic 'sophistication' and, consequently, has been exposed to more varieties of English simply by the fact that they are now older and have necessarily heard an increasing number of dialects. Eighth graders, on the other hand, would certainly be expected to have attained that degree of linguistic competence well beyond first graders' command of English and would also be expected to be more conscious of the relative importance of the influence speech has on another person's evaluation of a speaker.

When looking at the dynamics of the linguistic and cultural aspects of the North End ethnic community, which, in fact, have been shown to affect the speech of the Italian-American children, there is a reasonable explanation for the phenomenon that fourth graders, and not first graders, had the highest frequency rates of the socially stigmatized forms in all three styles. The fundamental reason is one grounded in a psychological phenomenon referred to as *peer group conformity*. We maintain that the results of the correlated linguistic and social variables support the basic hypothesis that peer group conformity is exerted on, felt by, and, consequently, reacted to most strongly by, both monolingual and bilingual children at around ten years of age or while in the fourth grade, than at age six (first grade) or at age fourteen (eighth grade).

The motivational base for conformity is commonly accepted as being at least twofold. Deutsch and Gerard (1955), for example, have proposed a distinction between normative and informational forms of social influence. *Normative* conformity is considered to be controlled primarily by a need or desire for group acceptance and/or a desire to avoid disapproval, whereas *informational* conformity is governed by a desire for information or a desire to be correct. The operation of these motivational systems is thought to vary with the task and the age of the child. The interaction of these motivational changes with the grade-age sociolinguistic correlations is being proposed here to account for the present results of the Italian-American children's varying frequencies of the stigmatized features.

The need for peer approval and the need to be correct are both thought by some psychologists (Allen 1965; Francescato 1970) to increase in strength with age. Moreover, the kinds of behavior that produce peer approval change with age. Mere conformity may be sufficient to gain peer approval only when it is compatible with the demands of objective correctness. Furthermore, with age, children are increasingly able to answer questions correctly and to determine if a correct answer is possible. These combined factors suggest at least a partial explanation for the findings of the sociolinguistic correlation among the three linguistic variables and the grade-age social variable.

When a North End child enters the first grade, he has been prepared by his parents, especially by his mother, to regard school as a place where he will meet other children his own age and learn how to do different interesting things like reading and writing, spelling and counting numbers. A child entering first grade begins to experience another form of the socialization process, one in which he learns to interact with other children in a more formal setting of the classroom.

Most first graders are open to experiencing a variety of unfamiliar things. They are enthusiastically eager to learn and are so amazingly malleable that they can be easily led by the teacher from the world of the unknown to that of the known. But first graders also bring with them to their very first day of school their linguistic competence which was developed up to that stage in their lives by what they have said and heard principally at home and in the streets and on the playgrounds. Therefore, their linguistic repertoires mirror their limited years of communicating with their parents, siblings, relatives, adult friends, and peers.

First graders tend to conform to what is thought to be good and correct by their parents, whom they judge to be foremost authorities on almost all issues, whether relevant or trivial. Long before entering school, these six-year-old Italian-American children have sought approval primarily from their parents, and only secondarily from their siblings and peers. First graders are less aware than fourth and eighth graders of the social implications of their speech. First graders are less aware of the differences between socially stigmatized and nonstigmatized linguistic forms. Generally speaking, first graders are just beginning to become aware of the fact that some older persons, especially their teachers, always seem to stress the importance of knowing the difference between what can be said (acceptable speech) and what cannot be said (unacceptable speech).

By way of contrast, at the opposite end of the age continuum, the majority of North End eighth grade children have moved further among Erikson's developmental maturation stages. Eighth graders are now facing many challenges of their identity stage. In describing the eight stages of man, Erikson points out that children similar to the North End eighth graders go through a period of personality adjustment while attempting to establish their identity.

> The integration now taking place in the form of ego identity is, as pointed out, more than the sum of the childhood identifications. It is the accrued experience of the ego's ability to integrate all identifications with the vicissitudes of the libido, with the aptitudes developed out of endowment, and with the opportunities offered in social roles. The sense of ego identity, then, is the accrued confidence that the inner sameness and continuity prepared in the past are matched by the sameness and continuity of one's meaning for others, as evidenced in the tangible promise of a career. (1963:261-262)

Among the North End children in the eighth grade, there is stronger need than before to be correct, independent, and integral young persons. Their dependence on peer approval is not as strong as it was when they were younger. They are now more consciously aware of the social consequences of their speech and actions. Moreover, they realize more profoundly than before that they alone are utlimately responsible for their potential educational achievements and careers. It is during this period of personality development that eighth graders find the need to take on the responsibilities of making many more correct decisions independent of peer approval or disapproval when the choice of the

8 Summary and conclusions / 133

peer group is obviously incorrect. Thus, there tends to be minimal conformity among eighth graders, compared with either fourth or first graders. Working with similar age groups in an experiment dealing with peer group conformity, Hoving et al. discovered similar results to those found among the three grade-age groups of the North End.

> In older subjects [eighth graders] we find a much stronger need to be correct coupled with the subject's presumed inability to gain peer approval for agreement when the apparent choice of the group is obviously incorrect. Hence the minimal conformity at older ages . . .
> It is important to note that it is the decrease in the ability of older subjects to gain peer approval for agreement when the group's choice is clearly wrong, plus the increased strength of the need to be correct, that is believed to be responsible for the decrease in conformity behavior with age. (Hoving et al. 1969:636)

Fourth graders in the North End, however, are at that point in their maturation development at which their needs for peer approval outweigh their needs to conform to what is socially acceptable as good or correct. They do not seem mature enough to put into correct perspective the consequences of their speech and actions. They seem not to act responsibly relative to when they were in the first grade. They have become so much more dependent on peer group approval that as a result whatever is needed to gain this approval dictates these ten-year-old children's speech and actions. Hence, the reason for the relatively large increase in the use of socially stigmatized forms in their speech. This large quantity of stigmatized forms insures peer group approval and continuing acceptance, since conformity behavior is highly regarded by insecure ten-year-old children. To avoid disapproval at practically all costs seems to become a guiding working principle during this developmental stage. It is a stage in their socialization development in which they are so overwhelmingly attached to peer group approval that as a result to use socially stigmatized forms in their speech is one way to identify with the iconoclastic, 'rough and tough guy' stereotype image which they seem to idealize. Erikson describes the dangers of this personality development stage as one reflecting children's strong feelings of inadequacy and inferiority.

> The child's danger, at this stage, lies in a sense of inadequacy and inferiority. If he despairs of his tools and skills or of his status among his tool partners, he may be discouraged from identification with them and with a section of the tool world. To lose the hope of such 'industrial' association may pull him back to the more isolated, less tool-conscious familial rivalry of the oedipal time . . . Many a child's development is disrupted when family life has failed to prepare him for school life, or when school fails to sustain the promises of earlier stages. (Erikson 1963:260)

In conclusion, then, it seems that in the course of the typical linguistic and socialization developments for most North End children, first graders use socially stigmatized forms with regularity, as do eighth graders. In marked contrast to either the first or eighth grade Italian-American children are the fourth grade children who in their maturation development seem to have become temporarily less confident in themselves during their socialization process. Fourth graders seem to have become so overly dependent and attached to peer group conformity that, as a result, they speak and act in ways which are compatible with group approval and acceptance. Apparently, one of the principal ways in which peer group conformity is achieved for many of the ten-year-old monolingual and bilingual children is through the usage of high frequencies of socially stigmatized forms. Therefore, it is hypothesized that by means of much higher frequencies of despirantization, consonant cluster simplification and Z_3 deletion, fourth graders express and insure their peer group solidarity.

When the three linguistic variables were correlated with the sexual identity social variable, males manifested a much stronger patterning of nonstandard usage than females in casual, narrative reading, and careful reading speech styles. This tendency for males to use the socially stigmatized speech forms much more often than females substantiated a number of previous studies regarding sexual identity related to nonstandard usage. The sexual identity social variable was one of the most consistent sociolinguistic patterns discovered in all of the North End data.

The ethnicity variable for the Italian-American children of the North End was not as consistently patterned as the two previous social variables of grade-age and sex. Although bilinguals had a lower rate of despirantization than monolinguals, for all practical purposes, bilinguals had an equivalent frequency to monolinguals for consonant cluster simplification. Moreover, when Z_3 deletion was correlated with ethnicity, bilinguals had a higher frequency of Z_3 absence than monolinguals. It is not entirely clear why this fluctuation in the sociolinguistic correlations of the three linguistic variables should occur. In general, it would be expected that bilinguals would have higher frequencies of despirantization than monolinguals since bilinguals' knowledge of Italian would cause interference problems when speaking English. However, one possible explanation for bilinguals' lower rate of despirantization lies in two interdependent factors: one linguistic and the other a sociohistorical factor. The first factor is that there are simply no voiced or voiceless interdental fricatives in Standard Italian nor in any of its variants; and the second factor is one rooted in the history of southern Italians immigrating to the North End.

Since the 1920s, the North End has been a vigorous ethnic community in which both newly arrived Italian immigrants and second and third generation Italian-Americans have lived and worked. For many Italian immigrants working and living in the North End, knowing how to speak English was not considered to be essential, since the vast majority of immigrant men were unskilled laborers who worked side by side with other Italian-speaking immigrants. Also, their foremen and bosses were frequently bilingual Italian-Americans. There was no apparent need to expend much time, effort, or money in learning English, since there was no urgent necessity to learn it. Their jobs did not depend on how well they spoke English. Similarly, immigrant women living in the North End did not experience any great necessity for knowing how to speak English, since they bought their food, clothing, and other merchandise from local Italian-speaking shopkeepers. Immigrant women who worked in nearby textile or candy factories often worked together with other immigrant Italian women. Their bilingual bosses gave them instructions in Italian. Thus, Italian, and not English, became the medium of communication for the vast majority of the North End residents.

When the need to speak English arose, however, Italian immigrants, with their minimal competence in English, would pronounce word-initial interdental fricatives such as *that* and *them*, and *three* and *think* with the closest Italian phonetic approximations, [d] and [t], respectively. Thus, English words exemplifying interdental fricatives in all three positions were despirantized. Moreover, the English which second generation Italian-American children first learned was English spoken and heard in the North End; it was *th*-less English. When second generation North End children heard English spoken, they often heard it spoken by Italian *immigrants* who generally despirantized interdental fricatives. Consequently, second generation children also adopted these non-standard features in their own dialects. As second generation Italian-American children went to grade school, and possibly to high school, they were necessarily taught how to pronounce words with Standard English pronunciation. Their non-North End teachers pronounced *th* words with Standard English interdental fricatives. Italian-American children were corrected by their teachers when they would pronounce *th* words with socially stigmatized //d// and //t//. As these second generation children grew up, some held jobs outside the North End while others went away to college or socialized with non-North Enders. Eventually, *th*-less English became less categorical and appeared more variably in the dialects of second and third generation Italian-Americans. However, there has never been an opportunity for despirantization to become totally absent in any generation living in the North End because of the ongoing influx of southern Italian immigrants coming to live in the North End. This influx of immigrants is one of the principal reasons inhibiting interdental fricatives from becoming realized categorically.

We can now return to the original question raised concerning the phenomenon that bilingual children indicated lower frequencies of despirantization than monolinguals. It is hypothesized that since bilingual children are more consciously aware that they speak differently from their monolingual peers and that their immigrant parents 'sound funny' when they speak English, bilingual children make more serious efforts than monolinguals in mastering Standard English pronunciations of interdental fricatives. In fact, bilinguals indicated in all administered tests that they are more conscious of the fact that despirantization is a highly marked stigmatized feature in Standard English. Furthermore, since bilingual children do not wish to appear too different from other American children, they have made more conscious efforts to develop the speech habit of pronouncing *th*-words with the appropriate voiced or voiceless interdental fricative.

    3. What is the influence of language attitudes and language usage on the Italian-American children's acculturation and socialization processes?

The North End of Boston is a geographically isolated enclave of over 12,000 people, 89.0 percent of whom are of Italian descent. Intermixed with second and third generation Italian-Americans are large numbers of immigrants. The speech community of the North End is heterogeneous since both Italian and English are spoken regularly. While Italian is the first language of many North End adults, it is also an acculturating language, since Italian spoken in Boston's North End has, over the last fifty years, taken on a number of phonological, lexical, and syntactic features of American English. Therefore, Italian spoken by immigrants in the North End has been so strongly affected by linguistic and cultural influences that North End Italian is obviously quite different from Italian spoken in southern Italy. But the dominant language spoken in the North End is English. Although bilingual children are required by their parents to develop competence in Italian, they, like their monolingual peers, are required by their schooling to develop competence in Standard English.

In Chapter 1, we described socialization as the process by which someone learns the ways of a given society or social group so that he can function within it. The process of socialization for North End children is not confined to infancy and childhood, but it obviously continues throughout the life cycle of the individual. Thus, the term socialization refers to learning new ways of the established and continuing Italian-American community in the North End. The Italian immigrant, child or adult, male or female, educated or ignorant, becomes socialized—perhaps slowly, but inevitably—within the American way of life. With the gradual acquisition of English, his socialization accelerates and becomes qualitatively transformed from its preverbal beginnings. Of course, English is part of the American heritage, and facility in the use of English is one of the kinds of competence toward which our American society directs its newborns and newly arrived immigrants.

While facility in English is one of the expected outcomes of the American socialization process, language acculturation is of enormous importance because it is one of the component processes of socialization long before full facility in English is achieved. Language acculturation is so important to understand because it is the process whereby a person, child or adult, learns the relevant rules of using a particular language so that communicative competence can be achieved. The data from various questionnaires, interviews, and participant observation all indicate that the principal variables that determine the process of the Italian-American children's acculturation and socialization are his basic motivations and role expectations, and the demands made upon him by those who live in the North End community. Since bilingual children speak both English and Italian, their social roles are not limited but even broader than those of monolingual children who are incapable of communicating in Italian. Bilingual children do not seem to have any noticeable difficulty in acquiring the new set of values and testing them out in relation to their new roles. Almost all of the North End monolingual and bilingual Italian-American children who were interviewed possess a healthy self-image of themselves, one that conforms to the one held by older Italian-Americans living in the North End. While bilingual children acculturate rapidly to the American way of life, there is no outright exchange of group identities. In other words, an immigrant child does not totally reject his inherited culture and language and then assume the life-style and language of Americans. It is important to note once again that both monolingual and bilingual children identify themselves as Italian-Americans, hyphenated persons sharing the values of both cultures.

As North End children acquire the linguistic system of American English, they also acquire a knowledge of the social world of rules for language use, such as when to talk, when to use polite forms, or when to be quiet. This type of knowledge has been referred to as communicative competence. It is suggested here that as monolingual and bilingual Italian-American children of the North End acquire English, they are also acquiring sociolinguistic perceptions which are a part of the socialization process. Such perceptions involve the knowledge that different people speak in different ways, that one kind of American English is thought of as better, and another kind of American English is thought of as worse. This type of social awareness of American English differences may indeed be thought of as part of an extended concept of communicative competence.

The character of the North End has made it an interesting, natural laboratory for the kind of sociolinguistic research undertaken there. The North End is typical of many ethnic enclaves in its makeup and yet it is limited enough to have made practical research possible. Its long history of Italian settlement with its present influx of immigrants enabled tests to be constructed, where language attitudes could be studied. Furthermore, not only are Italian-Americans an important group to study in terms of general principles of acculturation and socialization, but also they are a significant minority in their own right, and so the results of this study may prove somewhat helpful in better understanding the problems challenging the educators of monolingual and bilingual Italian-American children living in Boston's North End.

Appendix A: Questionnaires

Personal Data Information
 1. Name _____
 2. Address _____
 3. Telephone _____
 4. Sex _____
 5. Age _____
 6. Date of birth _____
 7. Place of birth _____
 8. If child was born in Italy, date of arrival to USA _____
 9. Name of school _____
 10. Present grade in school _____
 11. Mother's maiden name _____
 12. Mother's place of birth _____
 13. Mother's occupation _____
 14. Mother's completed level of education _____
 15. If mother was born in Italy, date of arrival to USA _____
 16. Father's name _____
 17. Father's place of birth _____
 18. Father's occupation _____
 19. Father's completed level of education _____
 20. If father was born in Italy, date of arrival to USA _____
 21. Brothers: Ages _____ _____ _____ _____
 22. Sisters: Ages _____ _____ _____ _____

Informant's Usage of Italian and English
 1. What language do you speak with your Mother and Father at home? _____
    1 2 3 4
 2. Do you ever speak in _____ (opposite language) with them? 1 2 3 4
 3. Whenever you go shopping with your Mother or Father to the grocery store or bakery in the neighborhood, and you want your Mother or Father to buy something you see you like, do you ask them to buy it for you in Italian ____ or in English ____ ? 1 2 3 4

4. Do you ever ask them to buy it for you in _____ (opposite language)? 1 2 3 4
5. Whenever you go downtown with your Mother or Father to one of the big department stores in Boston to shop or just walk around, do you speak to them in Italian ___ or in English ___ ? 1 2 3 4
6. Do you ever speak to them in _____ (opposite language)? 1 2 3 4
7. What language do your parents speak to one another in the house when you are there there inside the house? Italian ___ or English ___ . 1 2 3 4
8. Do you ever hear your parents speak in _____ (opposite language) when they think you are not listening to them or they think you are outside the house? Yes ___ or No ___ . 1 2 3 4
9. Do you understand your parents when they speak to you in Italian? Yes ___ or No ___ . 1 2 3 4
10. Can you understand your parents' English when they speak to you in English? Yes ___ or No ___ . 1 2 3 4
11. What language do you like to speak? Italian ___ or English ___? 1 2 3 4 Why? _____
12. Does either your Mother or Father speak to you in half Italian and half English? 1 2 3 4
13. Are there any special times when your Mother or Father always speak to you in Italian? Yes ___ or No ___ . When?
14. Are there any special times when your Mother or Father always speak to you in English? Yes ___ or No ___ . When?
15. Do you ever read any storybooks/comic books in Italian? 1 2 3 4
16. Do you ever read any storybooks/comic books in English? 1 2 3 4
17. Do you ever write in Italian, perhaps to some relatives in Italy? 1 2 3 4
18. When your relatives (aunts, uncles, grandparents) come to visit you and your family at your home, what language do they use to speak to your parents? Italian ___ or English ___ . 1 2 3 4
19. In speaking to you? Italian ___ or English ___ . 1 2 3 4
20. When your cousins about your own age come to visit you at your home, what language do they use with you? Italian ___ or English ___ . 1 2 3 4
21. Do you use this same language with your cousins? Yes ___ or No ___ . 1 2 3 4
22. Do you use this same language with your older relatives? Yes ___ or No ___ . 1 2 3 4
23. When you play with your cousins outside your house, do you speak in Italian ___ or in English ___ ? 1 2 3 4

24. To whom do you speak Italian besides your parents and relatives?
25. What language do you use when you speak to your brothers and sisters? Italian ___ or English ___ . 1 2 3 4
26. When do you use _____ (opposite language)?
27. What language do you use with the kids in the neighborhood when you play with them in the street or in the park? Italian ___ or English ___ . 1 2 3 4
28. When do you use _____ (opposite language)?
29. What language do you feel more comfortable in? Italian ___ or English ___. 1 2 3 4 Why?
30. When you get mad or get spanked by your parents, do you speak to your parents in Italian ___ or English ___ ? 1 2 3 4
31. How about when you get mad at your brothers or sisters or with kids in the neighborhood, what language do you use to yell back at them? Italian ___ or English ___ ? 1 2 3 4
32. When are you ashamed or embarrassed to speak Italian?
33. When are you ashamed or embarrassed to speak English?
34. Do you ever speak in Italian over the telephone? 1 2 3 4
35. When you say your prayers, like the 'Hail Mary' or the 'Our Father,' do you say them in Italian ___ or in English ___ ? 1 2 3 4
36. When you talk to Jesus privately and you tell him different things, do you remember what language you use? Italian ___ or English ___ . 1 2 3 4
37. Do you ever listen to a radio program in Italian or listen to Italian music on the radio? 1 2 3 4
38. When you go to confession, do you speak in Italian ___ or in English ___ ? 1 2 3 4
39. Do you ever tell any jokes in Italian? 1 2 3 4
40. If you had to choose to speak either Italian or English, what language would you choose? Italian ___ or English ___ . Why?

Language Maintenance and Shift Data

1. My best friends speak Italian. Yes ___ or No ___ .
2. My parents like me to say things to them in English at home. Yes ___ or No ___ .
3. My parents always make sure I do my homework. Yes ___ or No ___ .
4. Italian is a very difficult language. Yes ___ or No ___ .
5. My father is trying to learn English. Yes ___ or No ___ .

6. Someday I want to marry someone who speaks Italian. Yes ___ or No ___ .
7. My parents want me to learn English. Yes ___ or No ___ .
8. It's a good idea for me to know how to speak Italian. Yes ___ or No ___ .
9. American students should study Italian. Yes ___ or No ___ .
10. Later on in high school, I want to study French ___ , Spanish ___ , German ___ , Italian ___ .
11. My parents like me to say things to them in English at home. Yes ___ or No ___ .
12. It would be good if my teachers spoke to us students sometimes in Italian. Yes ___ or No ___ .
13. People who speak Italian are smart. Yes ___ or No ___ .
14. My parents want me to learn English. Yes ___ or No ___ .
15. If I had enough money, I would like to go to Italy and live there forever. Yes ___ or No ___ .
16. People who speak Italian are good. Yes ___ or No ___ .
17. The more American people I know, the more I want to learn how to speak English well. Yes ___ or No ___ .
18. My mother is trying to learn English. Yes ___ or No ___ .
19. Here in the North End of Boston, street signs should also be written in Italian. Yes ___ or No ___ .
20. If I should ever go to Italy, it will help me to know English. Yes ___ or No ___ .
21. Do Americans need to know Italian? Yes ___ or No ___ .
22. My parents like me to speak English with my brothers and sisters. Yes ___ or No ___ .
23. When I get married and raise a family, I want my own children to be able to speak Italian. Yes ___ or No ___ .
24. I am sometimes embarrassed or ashamed when other kids know that I can speak Italian. Yes ___ or No ___ .
25. My parents think that I should try to forget my Italian as quickly as possible. Yes ___ or No ___ .
26. I wish I could study Italian here at school. Yes ___ or No ___ .
27. There are advantages in understanding Italian and knowing how to speak Italian. Yes ___ or No ___ .
28. My parents like me to speak Italian with my brothers and sisters. Yes ___ or No ___ .

29. I am slowly forgetting my Italian. Yes ____ or No ____ .
30. Italian songs sound much better than American songs. Yes ____ or No ____ .
31. My parents encourage me to speak and to learn more Italian. Yes ____ or No ____ .
32. If I had the choice of knowing either Italian or English, I would rather know only English. Yes ____ or No ____ .
33. If I forget my Italian, it won't make much difference. Yes ____ or No ____ .

Elicitation of Narrative/Casual Speech

I. Games and leisure
 1. What are some of your favorite games you like to play?
 2. How do you play these games? What are the rules?
 3. What kind of games do you play at school or on the street?
 4. Do you have a pet at home? What kind?
 5. Do any of your friends have any pets?
 6. Have you ever gone to the zoo? What's your favorite animal?
 7. What are some of your favorite TV programs? Can you describe the last program you saw?
 8. What's the best movie you've ever seen? Can you tell me what it was all about?

II. School
 1. Tell me some of the things you like to do in class.
 2. Does your class ever go to museums on a field day?
 3. If yes, where, when, what have you seen?
 4. What *do* you like about St. Mary's/St. Anthony's/St. John's?
 5. What *don't* you like about St. Mary's/St. Anthony's/St. John's?
 6. What do you like to do on school holidays?
 7. What do you usually play after school?
 8. Where do you play after school?
 9. Do you have a teacher who hollers a lot?
 10. Are there any black kids in your class?

III. Aspirations
 1. What do you want to be when you grow up?
 2. How long does it take to be a _____ ?
 3. If you had all the money you wanted, what would you do with it?
 4. Would you travel? Where? Why?
 5. What famous person would you like to meet and be friends with?

IV. Special Occasions
   1. What's you favorite holiday?
   2. How does your family celebrate holidays like Christmas?
   3. Can you describe the summer festivals here in the North End?
   4. What do you like to do in the summer/winter months?
   5. Where did you go on a vacation last summer?

Reading

First Grade Selection

That Sam I am, that Sam I am.
I do not like that Sam I am.
Do you like green eggs and ham?
I do not like them Sam I am.
I do not like green eggs and ham.
Would you like them here or there?
I would not like them here or there.
I would not like them anywhere.
I do not like green eggs and ham.
I do not like them Sam I am.
Would you like them in a house?
Would you like them with a mouse?
I do not like them in a house.
I do not like them with a mouse.
I do not like them here or there.
I do not like them anywhere.
I do not like green eggs and ham.
I do not like them Sam I am.
Would you like them in a box?
Would you like them with a fox?
Not in a box,
Not with a fox,
Not in a house,
Not with a mouse.
I would not eat them here or there.
I would not eat them anywhere.
I would not eat green eggs and ham.
I do not like them Sam I am.
Would you? Could you in a car?
Eat them, eat them, here they are.
I would not, could not in a car.
You may like them, you will see.

You may like them in a tree.
I would not, could not in a tree.
Not in a car, you let me be!

Reprinted with permission, from: *Green Eggs and Ham*, by Dr. Seuss. Copyright © 1960. New York, Beginner Books, Inc. (a division of Random House).

Fourth Grade Selection

Mr. and Mrs. Kern have run the small shop on Sloan Street for many years. It is called the Swiss Bakery. They sell fresh homemade bread, delicious spice cakes, and all kinds of cookies. Mrs. Kern bakes everything herself in the kitchen of their home behind the store. Children in the neighborhood like to go to the bakery for their mothers, for Mrs. Kern always gives them a cookie. Although their prices are a little higher than those at the larger bakeries, the Kerns do a good business. They are known for always having fresh, high quality bakery products.

Reproduced from the Stanford Achievement Test, copyright ©1973, by Harcourt Brace Jovanovich, Inc. Reproduced by special permission of the publisher.

Eighth Grade Selection

Before a television picture can be broadcast, or telecast, it must be broken down into a series of tiny fragments. To get some idea of how a picture can be broken down in this manner, look closely at a newspaper picture. Note that this newspaper picture is made up of row after row of tiny dots. Some of the dots are large, some small. Many large dots together produce a dark area; small dots together produce a light area.

If every one of these dots were changed into an electric impulse (strong impulses for large dots and weak impulses for small dots), the first step in telecasting the picture would be made. Suppose that we call the instrument a 'dot changer.' To telecast the picture, the dot changer starts in the upper left-hand corner of the picture and moves across the top line of dots. As it comes to each dot in turn, the dot changer changes the dot into an electric impulse. If the dot is small, the impulse is small; if the dot is large, the impulse is large.

After the dot changer has scanned the first line of dots, it jumps to the left and starts across on the second line. This is the same way that your eyes move when you read a book. You read from left to right, moving down from line to line toward the bottom of the page.

As the dot changer thus changes one dot after another into an electric impulse, the receiver changes these electric impulses of varying strength into 'dots' of varying sizes. The action is so fast that the dots blend to produce a moving scene of the action that is going on in the television studio.

From Understanding Science (third edition), by William H. Crouse.
Copyright © 1963 by McGraw-Hill Book Company. Used with permission of McGraw-Hill Book Company.

Word-pair list of //ð//-//d// and //θ//-//t//

1. sky-fly
2. dog-frog
3. days-daze
4. boat-both
5. path-path
6. glue-glow
7. batroom-bathroom
8. then-den
9. those-doze
10. mother-mudder
11. wheat-wet
12. south-mouth
13. math-mat
14. this-dis
15. width-with
16. faith-fate
17. thy-thigh
18. boot-booth
19. these-those
20. rat-wrath
21. toot-tooth
22. pat-path
23. bite-bait
24. float-flop
25. faithful-fateful
26. thank-tank
27. book-bike
28. tin-thin
29. wit-with
30. willow-pillow
31. myth-mitt
32. width-with
33. boat-both
34. flop-flock
35. ask-ax
36. show-flow
37. north-nort
38. myth-mid
39. three-tree
40. pat-path

Name _____   Total errors _____

Instructions for Perception-Discrimination Test

You will hear a pair of words. Listen very carefully to the pair or set of two words and try to decide if the pair of two words sound the *same* or sound *different*. [pause] For example, 'cat' and 'cat' sound the *same*, but 'cat' and 'bat' sound *different*.

After each number, circle the letter *S* (which stands for 'same') if the two words sound the *same*, or circle the letter *D* (which stands for *different*) if the two words sound different from one another.

Do you understand these instructions? [pause]
Now listen very carefully. Ready? [pause]
[play tape]

Answer Sheet for Perception-Discrimination Test

1.	S D		21.	S D	
2.	S D		22.	S D	
3.	S D		23.	S D	
4.	S D		24.	S D	
5.	S D		25.	S D	
6.	S D		26.	S D	
7.	S D		27.	S D	
8.	S D		28.	S D	
9.	S D		29.	S D	
10.	S D		30.	S D	
11.	S D		31.	S D	
12.	S D		32.	S D	
13.	S D		33.	S D	
14.	S D		34.	S D	
15.	S D		35.	S D	
16.	S D		36.	S D	
17.	S D		37.	S D	
18.	S D		38.	S D	
19.	S D		39.	S D	
20.	S D		40.	S D	

Name _____ Total errors _____

Language Attitudes Test

Name _____ School _____ Grade ____ Age ____
   1. Is Speaker 1 a *boy* or a *girl*? (Circle your answer)
   2. What grade in school is Speaker 1? _____
   3. Is Speaker 1 *black* or *white*? (Circle your answer)
   4. Is Speaker 1 from our North End area? *Yes — No*
   5. Does he/she sound as if he/she was born in Italy? *Yes — No*
   6. How old do you think Speaker 1 is? _____

Speaker 1:
   7. has a *bad* or *nice* voice.
   8. speaks *fast* or *slow*.
   9. is a *good* or *bad* person.
   10. sounds *dumb* or *smart*.
   11. sounds *happy* or *sad*.
   12. sounds *ugly* or *nice*.
   13. sounds *calm* or *scared*.
   14. sounds *friendly* or *unfriendly*.
   15. is *older* or *younger* than you.

16. speaks *with* or *without* an Italian accent.
17. sounds *lazy* or *energetic*.
18. sounds *comfortable* or *uncomfortable*.
19. sounds like a *cold* or *warm* person.
20. is *easy* or *hard* to understand.
21. sounds *honest* or *dishonest*.

Appendix B: List of Speakers

Informants

Speaker no.	Grade	Sex	Ethnicity
01	first	male	bilingual
02	first	male	bilingual
03	first	male	bilingual
04	first	male	bilingual
05	first	male	bilingual
06	first	female	bilingual
07	first	female	bilingual
08	first	female	bilingual
09	first	female	bilingual
10	first	female	bilingual
11	first	male	monolingual
12	first	male	monolingual
13	first	male	monolingual
14	first	male	monolingual
15	first	male	monolingual
16	first	female	monolingual
17	first	female	monolingual
18	first	female	monolingual
19	first	female	monolingual
20	first	female	monolingual
21	fourth	male	bilingual
22	fourth	male	bilingual
23	fourth	male	bilingual
24	fourth	male	bilingual
25	fourth	male	bilingual
26	fourth	female	bilingual
27	fourth	female	bilingual
28	fourth	female	bilingual
29	fourth	female	bilingual
30	fourth	female	bilingual
31	fourth	male	monolingual

32	fourth	male	monolingual
33	fourth	male	monolingual
34	fourth	male	monolingual
35	fourth	male	monolingual
36	fourth	female	monolingual
37	fourth	female	monolingual
38	fourth	female	monolingual
39	fourth	female	monolingual
40	fourth	female	monolingual
41	eighth	male	bilingual
42	eighth	male	bilingual
43	eighth	male	bilingual
44	eighth	male	bilingual
45	eighth	male	bilingual
46	eighth	female	bilingual
47	eighth	female	bilingual
48	eighth	female	bilingual
49	eighth	female	bilingual
50	eighth	female	bilingual
51	eighth	male	monolingual
52	eighth	male	monolingual
53	eighth	male	monolingual
54	eighth	male	monolingual
55	eighth	male	monolingual
56	eighth	female	monolingual
57	eighth	female	monolingual
58	eighth	female	monolingual
59	eighth	female	monolingual
60	eighth	female	monolingual

Notes

1. In order to have assumed a common, objective, and measureable standard within the speech setting, the first minute of recorded speech of each informant was disregarded as potential linguistic data. There were various reasons grounding this decision: the possibility of the informant experiencing nervousness, embarrassment, or insecurity of the speech setting. Any of these emotionally based situations could have inhibited the linguistically desirable spontaneous speech samples from the Italian-American children of the North End.

2. The example of word-initial voiceless *th-* which occurred only once in the fourth grade reading selection was *everything*. The reasons for treating the class of words such as *(every)thing, (any)thing, (some)thing,* and *(no)thing* have already been discussed in this chapter. Therefore, it was decided that *everything* should not be analyzed as an example of word-medial voiceless *-th-* but rather as word-initial voiceless *th-*.

3. The results of the perception-discrimination test indicated that there were only three of the sixty informants (two in the first grade and one in the fourth grade) whose responses were mismatched in either # # (4) and (33); (22) and (40).

4. The following word-pairs were omitted from the list because they do not contain the minimal difference reflecting the standard and nonstandard variants of //ð//-//d// and //θ//-//t//: (12) *south-mouth*; (15) and (32) *width-with*; (17) *thy-thigh*; (19) *these-those*; and (38) *myth-mid*.

5. The analysis of the responses to the Informant's Usage of Italian and English questionnaire yielded more refined information than merely the percentages of affirmative and negative answers for each item in the questionnaire. For the majority of the questions, each informant was asked to respond by choosing one of four possible answers: (1) always; (2) most of the time; (3) sometimes, but not very often; (4) never. The researcher would circle the appropriate number representing the answer given by the informant.

References

Allen, V. L., 1965. Situational factors in conformity. In: Advances in experimental social psychology. Ed. by L. Berkowitz. New York, Academic Press.

Anisfeld, M. and W. E. Lambert. 1964. Evaluational reactions of bilingual and monolingual children to spoken languages. Journal of abnormal and social psychology. 69. 89-97.

―――――, N. Bogo and W. E. Lambert. 1962. Evaluational reactions to accepted English speech. Journal of abnormal and social psychology. 65. 223-31.

Argyle, M. 1957. Social pressure in public and private situations. Journal of abnormal and social psychology. 54. 172-75.

Arnold, D. B. 1961. Linguistic variation in a New England community. Unpublished Ph.D. dissertation. Cambridge, Harvard University.

Asch, S. E. 1956. Studies of independence and conformity: A minority of one against a unanimous majority. Psychological monographs. 70. 9.

Bailey, C-J. N. 1972. The patterning of language variation. In: Varieties of present-day English. Ed. by R. W. Bailey and J. L. Robinson. New York, Macmillan.

―――――, 1973. Variation and linguistic theory. Washington, D.C., Center for Applied Linguistics.

―――――, and R. W. Shuy, eds. 1973. New ways of analyzing variation in English. Washington, D.C., Georgetown University Press.

Banfield, E. C. 1958. The moral basis of a backward society. Glencoe, Free Press.

Baratz, J. C. and R. W. Shuy, eds. 1969. Teaching black children to read. Washington, D.C., Center for Applied Linguistics.

Berenda, R. W. 1950. The influence of the group on the judgments of children. New York, Kings Crown Press.

Berko-Gleason, J. 1971. Code switching in children's language. Paper read at LSA Institute. Buffalo, N.Y.

Bernstein, B. 1968. Some sociological determinants of perception: An inquiry into subcultural differences. In: Readings in the sociology of language. Ed. by J. A. Fishman, 223-39. The Hague, Mouton.

Bickerton, D. 1971. Inherent variability and variable rules. Foundations of language. 7. 457-92.
Bock, P. K. 1968. Social structure and language structure. In: Readings in the sociology of language. Ed. by J. A. Fishman, 212-22. The Hague, Mouton.
Bouchard-Ryan, E. L. 1969. Psycholinguistic attitude study. In: Studies in language and language behavior, Progress report no. 7. Center for Research on Language and Behavior. The University of Michigan.
———. 1973. Subjective reactions toward accented speech. In: Language attitudes: Current trends and prospects. Ed. by R. W. Shuy and R. W. Fasold, 60-73. Washington, D.C., Georgetown University Press.
Bourhis, R. Y., H. Giles and W. E. Lambert. 1972. Social consequences of accommodating one's style of speech: A cross national investigation. Unpublished manuscript.
Brown, B. L. 1969. The social psychology of variations in French Canadian speech styles. Unpublished Ph.D. dissertation. Montreal, McGill University.
Campisi, P. J. 1948. Ethnic family patterns: The Italian family in United States. American journal of sociology. 33. 443-49.
Cardarelli, A. P. 1972. Crime in Boston: An analysis of the serious crime patterns in 81 neighborhoods. Office of Public Relations, Boston Metropolitan Police Department, Boston. Mimeographed 1-25.
Carrea-Zoli, Y. 1970. Lexical and morphological aspects of American-Italians in San Francisco. Unpublished Ph.D. dissertation. Stanford, Stanford University.
Cedergren, H. J. and D. Sankoff. 1972. Variable rules: Performance as a statistical reflection of competence. Unpublished manuscript.
Child, I. 1943. Italian or American? The second generation in conflict. New Haven, Yale University Press.
Chomsky, N. 1965. Aspects of the theory of syntax. Cambridge, The M.I.T. Press.
——— and M. Halle. 1968. The sound pattern of English. New York, Harper and Row.
Cohen, A. 1972. Language attitudes of Mexican-American parents and teenagers in Redwood City, California. Prepared for First Annual Faculty—Student Seminar, Tri-University Training Program in Language and Social Change. Topic: Language Attitudes. Yeshiva University, New York City. Mimeographed.
Costanzo, P. R. and M. E. Shaw. 1966. Conformity as a function of age level. Child development. 37. 967-75.
Covello, Leonard. 1967. The social background of the Italo-American school child. Leiden, E. J. Brill.
———. 1970. The teacher in the urban community: A half century in city schools. New York, Littlefield and Adams.
Crutchfield, R. S. 1955. Conformity and character. American psychologist. 10. 191-98.
d'Anglejan, A. and G. R. Tucker. 1973. Sociolinguistic correlates of speech style in Quebec. In: Language attitudes: Current trends and prospects. Ed. by R.

W. Shuy and R. W. Fasold, 1-27. Washington, D.C., Georgetown University Press.

DeConde, A. 1971. Half bitter, half sweet: An excursion into Italian-American history. New York, Scribner.

DeStephano, J. S. 1972. The development of a formal register in Black children's language. Paper read at the Fourth Triennial Conference of Symbolic Processes. Washington, D.C., April.

Deutsch, M. D. and H. B. Gerard. 1955. A study of normative and informational social influence upon individual judgment. Journal of abnormal and social psychology. 51. 629-36.

Duke, F. J. 1938. A phonetic study of Italo-American speech in Richmond, Virginia. Unpublished Ph.D. dissertation. Richmond, University of Virginia.

Dunn, E. 1973. Four areas of Boston, 1970: A report based on the 1970 census: III North City. United Community Services of Metropolitan Boston, Boston. 1-29.

Dwyer, D. and D. M. Smith. 1967. An introduction to West African Pidgin English. East Lansing, Michigan State University Press.

Ellis, D. S. 1967. Speech and social status in America. Social forces. 45. 431-37.

Erikson, Erik H. 1963. Childhood and society. New York, W. W. Norton.

―――. 1968. Identity, youth, and crisis. New York, W. W. Norton.

Ervin-Tripp, S. M. 1971. Social dialects in developmental sociolinguistics. In: Sociolinguistics: A cross disciplinary perspective. Washington, D.C., Georgetown University Press.

Fasold, R. W. 1969. Tense and the form *be* in Black English. Lg. 45. 763-76.

―――. 1970. Two models of socially significant linguistic variation. Lg. 46. 551-63.

―――. 1972. Tense marking in Black English: A linguistic and social analysis. Washington, Center for Applied Linguistics.

――― and W. Wolfram. 1970. Some linguistic features of Negro dialect. In: Teaching standard English in the inner city. Ed. by R. W. Fasold and R. W. Shuy, 41-86. Washington, D.C., Center for Applied Linguistics.

Ferroni, C. D. 1969. The Italians in Cleveland: A study in assimilation. Unpublished Ph.D. dissertation. Kent, Kent State University.

Firey, W. I. 1947. Land use in central Boston. Cambridge, Harvard University Press.

Fishman, J. A. 1966. Language loyalty in the United States. The Hague, Mouton.

―――. 1969. Bilingual attitudes and behaviors. Language sciences. April. 5-11.

―――. 1972. Language in sociocultural change: Essays by Joshua A. Fishman. Selected and introduced by A. S. Dil. Stanford, Stanford University Press.

Fodale, P. 1964. The Sicilian dialects as a diasystem: A study in structural dialectology. Unpublished Ph.D. dissertation. Ann Arbor, University of Michigan.

Foerster, R. 1932. Italian emigration of our times. Cambridge, Harvard University Press.
Francescato, G. 1970. Il linguaggio del bambino: problemi di psicologia. Milano, Nuova Italia.
Gallo, P. J. 1974. Ethnic alientation: The Italian-Americans. Cranbury, N.J., Fairleigh Dickinson University Press.
Gambino, R. 1972. Myth called the Mafia puts Italian-Americans in dilemma. Boston Globe, 30 April, sec. B, 72.
_____. 1974. Blood of my blood: The dilemma of the Italian-Americans. Garden City, Doubleday.
Gans, H. J. 1962. The urban villagers: Group and class life of Italian-Americans. New York, Free Press.
Giacosa, G. 1892. Gli italiani a New York e a Chicago. Nuova antologia. 124. 619-40.
Giles, H. 1970. Evaluative reactions to accents. Educational review. 22. 211-27.
_____. 1971a. Patterns of evaluation to R. P., South Welsh, and Somerset accented speech. British journal of social and clinical psychology. 10. 280-1.
_____. 1971b. Ethnocentrism and the evaluation of accented speech. British journal of social and clinical psychology. 10. 187-81.
_____. 1971c. Our reactions to accent. New society. 14. 713-15.
Girardon, M. 1949. La lingua dello yesse in USA. Nuova antologia. 446. 68-89.
Gisolfi, A. 1939. Italian-American: What it has borrowed from American English and what it is contributing to the American language. Commonwealth. 3. 21-30.
Glazer, N. and D. P. Moynihan. 1963. Beyond the melting pot. Cambridge, Harvard University Press.
Gleason, H. A. 1961. An introduction to descriptive linguistics. New York, Holt, Rinehart, Winston.
Goodman, M. E. 1952. Race-awareness in young children. Addison, Wesley Press.
Grasso, P. G. 1964. Personalità giovanile in transizione dal familismo al personalismo: Ricerca psicosociologica su giovani emigrati. Zurich, Pas-Verlag.
Grossman, R. P. 1966. The Italians in America. Minneapolis, Lerner.
Gumperz, J. J. and D. Hymes, eds. 1972. Directions in sociolinguistics: The ethnography of communication. New York, Holt, Rinehart, and Winston.
Halle, M. 1962. Phonology in generative grammar. Word 18. 54-72.
Handlin, O. 1952. The uprooted. Boston, Little Brown.
_____. 1966. Children of the uprooted. New York, Doubleday.
Hansen, M. L. 1948. The immigrant in American history. Cambridge, Harvard University Press.
Harms, L. S. 1961. Listener judgments of status cues in speech. Quarterly journal of speech. 47. 164-8.

———. 1963. Status cues in speech: Extra-race and extra-region identification. Lingua 12. 300-6.
Hoving, K. L., N. H. Hamm, and K. Roehl. 1967. Conformity in children as a function of adult vs. peer influence hypothetical vs. real model and degree of perceptual ambiguity. Paper presented at the meeting of the Society for Research in Child Development, New York.
———, N. Hamm, and P. Galvin. 1969. Social influence as a function of stimulus ambiguity at three age levels. Developmental psychology. 1. 631-6.
Hymes, D. H. 1968. The ethnography of speaking. In: Readings in the sociology of language. Ed. by J. A. Fishman, 99-138. The Hague, Mouton.
———. 1971. Competence and performance in linguistic theory. In: Language acquisition: Models and methods. Ed. by R. Huxley and E. Ingram, 3-28. New York, Academic Press.
———. 1971. Pidginization and creolization of languages. Cambridge, Cambridge University Press.
———. 1972. Towards communicative competence. Philadelphia, University of Pennsylvania Press.
Iorizzo, L. J. and S. Mondello. 1970. The Italian-Americans. New York, Twayne.
King, R. D. 1969. Historical linguistics and generative grammar. Englewood Cliffs, N.J., Prentice-Hall.
Kiparsky, P. 1968. Linguistic universals and linguistic change. In: Universals in linguistic theory. Ed. by E. Bach and R. Harms. New York, Holt, Rinehart, Winston.
Labov, W. 1965. On the mechanism of linguistic change. In: Georgetown University Round Table on Languages and Linguistics 1965. Ed. by C. W. Kreidler. Washington, D.C., Georgetown University Press.
———. 1966. The social stratification of English in New York City. Washington, D.C., Center for Applied Linguistics.
———. 1967. The effect of social mobility on linguistic behavior. In: Explorations in sociolinguistics. Ed. by S. Lieberson, 58-75. The Hague, Mouton.
———. 1969. Contraction, deletion, and inherent variability of the English copula. Lg. 45. 715-62.
———. 1972a. Some principles of linguistic methodology. Language in society. 1. 97-120.
———. 1972b. Language in the inner city: Studies in the Black English vernacular. Philadelphia, University of Pennsylvania Press.
———. 1972c. Sociolinguistic patterns. Philadelphia, University of Pennsylvania Press.
———, P. Cohen, C. Robins, and J. Lewis. 1968. A study of the non-standard English of Negro and Puerto Rican speakers in New York City. USOE Final Report, Research Project 3288.

Lambert, W. E. 1967. A social psychology of bilingualism. The journal of social issues. 23. 91-109.
———, M. Anisfeld, and G. Yeni-Komshian. 1965. Evaluational reactions of Jewish and Arab adolescents to dialect and language variation. Journal of personality and social psychology. 2. 85-90.
———, H. Frankel, and G. R. Tucker. 1966. Judging personality through speech: A French-Canadian example. Journal of communication. 16. 305-21.
———, R. C. Hodgson, R. C. Gardner, and S. Fillenbaum. 1960. Evaluational reactions to spoken languages. Journal of abnormal psychology. 60. 44-51.
Lopreato, Joseph. 1970. The Italian-Americans. New York, Random House.
MacDonald, J. S. and B. MacDonald. 1962. Urbanization, ethnic groups and social segmentation. Social research. 29. 433-48.
Markel, N. N., R. M. Eisler, and H. W. Reese. 1967. Judging personality from dialect. Journal of verbal learning and verbal behavior. 6. 33-4.
Merton, R. K. 1968. Social theory and social structure. New York, Free Press.
Miller, L. M. 1972. Evaluational reactions of Mexican-American and Anglo teachers to children's speech. Western speech. 36. 104-14.
Moquin, W. and C. Van Doren. 1974. A documentary history of the Italian-Americans. New York, Praeger.
Nader, L. 1968. A note on attitudes and the use of language. In: Readings in the sociology of language. Ed. by J. A. Fishman, 276-81. The Hague, Mouton.
Nelli, H. S. 1970. Italians in urban America. In: The experience in the United States. Ed. by M. H. Engel and S. M. Tomasi. Staten Island, N.Y., Center for Migration Studies.
Novak, M. 1972. The rise of the unmeltable ethnics. New York, Macmillan.
Osgood, C. E. 1964. Semantic differential technique in the comparative study of cultures. American anthropologist. 66. 171-200.
Osser, H., M. Wand, and F. Zaid. 1969. The young child's ability to imitate and comprehend speech: A comparison of two subcultural groups. Child development. 40. 1063-76.
Palisi, L. E. 1966. Ethnic generation and family structure. Journal of marriage and family. 28. 49-50.
Palmer, L. A. 1973. A preliminary report on a study of the linguistic correlates or raters' subjective judgments of non-native English speech. In: Language attitudes: Current trends and prospects. Ed. by R. W. Shuy and R. W. Fasold, 41-59. Washington, D.C., Georgetown University Press.
Parenti, M. J. 1962. Ethnic and political attitudes: A depth study of Italian-Americans. Unpublished Ph.D. dissertation. New Haven, Yale University.
Psathas, G. 1957. Ethnicity, social class and adolescent independence from parental control. American sociological review. 22. 415-23.
Reed, C. E. 1967. Dialects of American English. New York, World Publishing Company.

Reitan, H. T. and M. E. Shaw. 1964. Group membership, sex composition of the group, and conformity behavior. Journal of social psychology. 64. 45-51.
Rey, A. 1974. A study of the attitudinal effect of a Spanish accent on Blacks and Whites in south Florida. Unpublished Ph.D. dissertation. Washington, D.C., Georgetown University.
Rosenthal, M. 1974. The acquisition of children's awareness of language differences. Unpublished Ph.D. dissertation. Washington, D.C., Georgetown University.
Russo, N. J. 1970. Three generations of Italians in New York City: Their religious acculturation. In: The Italian experience in the United States. Ed. by M. H. Engel and S. Tomasi. Staten Island, N.Y., Center for Migration Studies.
Sankoff, G. 1972. A quantitative paradigm for the study of communicative competence. Paper read at the Conference on the Ethnography of Speaking. University of Texas.
———— and P. Kay. 1972. A language-universals approach to pidgins and creoles. Paper read at the 23rd Round Table on Languages and Linguistics, Georgetown University, Washington, D.C.
Schneider, F. 1970. Conforming behavior of black and white children. Journal of personality and social psychology. 13. 466-71.
Schumann, F. 1972. Preliminary investigation into the sociolinguistic attitudes of Cambridge Portuguese students. Mimeographed.
Seligman, C. R., G. R. Tucker, and W. E. Lambert. 1972. The effects of speech style and other attributes on teacher's attitudes towards pupils. Language in society. 1. 131-42.
Seuss, Dr. 1960. Green eggs and ham. New York, Beginner Books.
Shibutani, T. and K. Kwan. 1965. Ethnic stratification. New York, Macmillan.
Shuy, R. W. 1967. Discovering American dialects. Champaign, Ill., National Council of Teachers of English.
————. 1969. Subjective judgments in sociolinguistic analysis. Georgetown University Round Table on Languages and Linguistics 1969. Ed. by J. E. Alatis. 175-88. Washington, D.C., Georgetown University Press.
————. 1972. Sociolinguistics and teacher attitudes in a southern school system. In: Sociolinguistics in cross-cultural analysis. Ed. by D. M. Smith and R. W. Shuy, 67-82. Washington, D.C., Georgetown University Press.
————, J. C. Baratz, and W. A. Wolfram. 1970. Sociolinguistic factors in speech identification. Washington, D.C., Center for Applied Linguistics.
———— and F. Williams. 1973. Stereotyped attitudes of selected English dialect communities. In: Language attitudes: Current trends and prospects. Ed. by R. W. Shuy and R. W. Fasold, 85-96. Washington, D.C., Georgetown University Press.
———— and R. W. Fasold. 1971. Contemporary emphases in linguistics. Georgetown University Round Table on Languages and Linguistics 1971. Ed.

by R. J. O'Brien, S.J. 185-97. Washington, D.C., Georgetown University Press.

───── , W. A. Wolfram, and W. K. Riley. 1968. Linguistic correlates of social stratification in Detroit speech. Washington, D.C., Center for Applied Linguistics.

Simoncini, F. 1959. The San Francisco dialect—a study. Orbis. 8. 342-54.

Slobin, D. I. et al. 1967. A field manual for cross-cultural study of the acquisition of communicative competence. Berkeley, University of California.

Smith, D. M. 1972a. Language as social adaptation. In: Languages and linguistics working papers. No. 4. Ed. by R. J. O'Brien, S.J. Washington, D.C., Georgetown University Press.

───── . 1972b. Some implications for the social status of pidgin languages. In: Sociolinguistics in cross-cultural analysis. Ed. by D. M. Smith and R. W. Shuy. Washington, D.C., Georgetown University Press.

───── . 1973a. Language, speech, and ideology: A conceptual framework. In: Language attitudes: Current trends and prospects. Ed. by R. W. Shuy and R. W. Fasold. Washington, D.C., Georgetown University Press.

───── . 1973b. Creolization and language ontogeny. In: New ways of analyzing variation in English. Ed. by C-J. N. Bailey and R. W. Shuy. Washington, D.C., Georgetown University Press.

Stewart, W.A. 1967. Sociolinguistic factors in the history of American Negro dialects. The Florida FL Reporter. 5 (Spring). 11, 22, 24, 26.

───── . 1968. Continuity and change in American Negro dialects. The Florida FL Reporter. 6 (Spring). 14-16, 18, 304.

Ticho, G. R. 1971. Cultural aspects of transference and countertransference. Bulletin of the Menninger clinic. 35. 7-20.

Tomasi, S. M. 1970. The ethnic church and the integration of Italian immigrants in the United States. In: The Italian experience in the United States. Ed. by M. H. Engel and S. M. Tomasi. Staten Island, N.Y., Center for Migration Studies.

Tramontozzi, L. 1972. Can Italian power save the North End? Boston Magazine 12 (October) 56-73.

Traugott, E. 1972. Lectures on historical linguistics and its relation to studies of language acquisition and pidgins and creoles. University of California at Santa Cruz, Summer Program in Linguistics.

Tucker, G. R. 1968. Judging personality from language use: A Filipino example. Philippine sociological review. 16. 30-39.

───── and W. E. Lambert. 1969. White and Negro listeners' reactions to various American English dialects. Social forces. 47. 463-8.

U.S. Bureau of the Census. 1972. Census of population and housing: 1970 census tracts, final report PHC (1) 29, Boston, Massachusetts, SMSA. Washington, D.C., Government Printing Office.

Vecoli, R. 1969. Prelates and peasants: Italian immigrants and the Catholic church. Journal of social history. (Spring) 217-68.

Weinreich, U. 1966. Languages in contact. The Hague, Mouton.

———, W. Labov, and M. Herzog. 1968. Empirical foundations for a theory of language change. In: Directions for historical linguistics. Ed. by W. P. Lehman. Austin, University of Texas Press.

Weisberg, J. 1962. Views of the News—Jews of the North End. Jewish Advocate. 5 April, sec. A 1. Boston.

Wenk, M., S. M. Tomasi, and G. Baroni. 1972. Pieces of a dream. New York, Center for Migration Studies.

Wheeler, T. C. 1971. The immigrant experience: The anguish of becoming American. New York, Dial Press.

Whitehead, J. L. and L. Miller. 1972. Correspondence between evaluations of children's speech anticipated upon the basis of stereotype. Southern speech communications journal. 37. 375-86.

Whyte, W. 1939. Race conflict in the North End of Boston. New England quarterly. 12. 623-42.

———. 1967. Street corner society. Chicago, University of Chicago.

Williams, F. 1970a. Language, attitude, and social change. In: Language and poverty: Perspectives on a theme. Ed. by F. Williams. Chicago, Markham.

———. 1970b. Psychological correlates of speech characteristics: On sounding 'disadvantaged'. Journal of speech and hearing research. 13. 472-88.

———, J. L. Whitehead, and L. M. Miller. 1971a. Attitudinal correlates of children's speech characteristics. USOE Research Report Project No. 0-0336.

———. 1971b. Ethnic stereotyping and judgments of children's speech. Speech monographs 38. 166-70.

———, J. L. Whitehead, and J. Traupmann. 1971. Teachers' evaluations of children's speech. Speech teacher. 20. 247-54.

———, J. L. Whitehead, and L. M. Miller. 1972. Relations between language attitudes and teacher expectancy. American educational research journal. 17. 47-56.

——— and W. A. Shamo. 1972. Regional variations in teachers' attitudes toward children's language. Central States speech journal.

———. 1973. Some research notes on dialect attitudes and stereotypes. In: Language attitudes: Current trends and prospects. Ed. by R. W. Shuy and R. W. Fasold. Washington, D.C., Georgetown University Press.

Williams, P. 1938. Southern Italian folkways in Europe and America. New Haven, Yale University Press.

Wölck, W. 1973. Attitudes toward Spanish and Quechua in bilingual Peru. In: Language attitudes: Current trends and prospects. Ed. by R. W. Shuy and R. W. Fasold. Washington, D.C., Georgetown University Press.

Wolff, H. 1959. Intelligibility and inter-ethnic attitudes. Anthropological linguistics. Vol. P (3) 34-41.

———. 1964. Intelligibility and inter-ethnic attitudes. In: Language and culture and society: A reader in linguistics and anthropology. Ed. by D. Hymes. New York, Harper and Row.

Wolfram, W. A. 1969. A sociolinguistic description of Detroit Negro speech. Washington, D.C., Center for Applied Linguistics.
_____. 1974. Overlapping influence in the English of second generation Puerto Rican teenagers in East Harlem. Arlington, Va., Center for Applied Linguistics.
_____ and R. W. Fasold. 1970. Some linguistic features of Negro dialect. In: Teaching standard English in the inner city. Ed. by R. W. Fasold and R. W. Shuy, 41-86. Washington, D.C., Center for Applied Linguistics.
Yarrow, M. R. 1958. Personality development and minority group membership. In: The Jews: Social patterns of an American group. Ed. by M. Sklare. New York, Free Press.